PHILOSOPHY FOR PLEASURE

PHILOSOPHY
FOR
PLEASURE

BY

HECTOR HAWTON

LONDON

WATTS & CO.

5 & 6 JOHNSON'S COURT, FLEET STREET, E.C.4

First published 1949
Second impression 1952

*Printed in Great Britain by Richard Clay and Co. Ltd.,
Bungay, Suffolk, and published by C. A. Watts and Co. Ltd.,
5 and 6 Johnson's Court, Fleet Street, London, E.C.4*

TO

ERICA
TO WHOM I OWE
SO MUCH

Contents

	INTRODUCTION	ix
I	WHAT PHILOSOPHY IS ABOUT	1
II	THE DISCOVERY OF REASON	13
III	THE RAPE OF REASON	27
IV	ARCHITECTS OF THE UNIVERSE	38
V	THE REVOLT AGAINST METAPHYSICS	52
VI	THE GREAT DILEMMA	65
VII	THE KANTIAN COMPROMISE	82
VIII	THE RETURN TO METAPHYSICS	100
IX	THE AFTERMATH OF HEGEL	117
X	THE UNIVERSE OF SCIENCE	134
XI	THE PROBLEM OF CHANGE	149
XII	THE NEW LOGIC	167
XIII	THE DEBATE CONTINUES	186
	GLOSSARY OF TERMS	202
	TABLE OF DATES	207
	INDEX	209

Introduction

By

PROF. A. E. HEATH

WHEN I had finished reading the manuscript of this book I came to the reluctant conclusion that Mr. Hector Hawton, though not an academic person, had beaten the professional philosophers at their own game. How? Not because his book is the result of wide and careful reading of philosophical authors. It *is* that, but there are plenty of such studies already—in varying degrees of readability. It was because this harvested material has been passed through a clear and critical mind, and then presented with freshness and vivacity. The title of the book, *Philosophy for Pleasure*, has real point.

Both men of science and philosophers know that wide learning is only too readily harnessed to prejudice. That is why the gifted amateur, the outsider, often sees most of the game. In my opinion Mr. Hawton's book is an excellent example of this. To his training in the discipline of writing he adds a restless interest in things of the mind : and, not being overwhelmed by authority of great names, he succeeds in seeing the wood in spite of the trees. Too often books on philosophy give the impression that there are as many philosophies as there are philosophers. But, as Mr. Hawton rightly says, " It is quite wrong to suppose that a history of philosophy resembles a vast Brains Trust, and that students must sit back and listen to the opinions of Plato, Descartes, Locke, Kant, and so on." These outstanding men are much more than writers to be read : they are, every one of them, examples of a centuries-old and sustained attempt to frame, in ever clearer and more subtle language, those fundamental *questions* which we are all (in our more reflective moments) forced to ask ourselves.

This mode of approach to philosophical studies enables Mr. Hawton to present philosophy as a perpetual adventure in the world of ideas. We know that the chief glory of science is that it is never finished, because the wider the sphere of knowledge grows the larger is its area of contact with the unknown. In philosophy, too, the unending struggle goes on. My own personal view is that philosophy is not a subject of study, but a way of studying all subjects.

Mr. Hawton adopts a similar attitude, and so is able, in this little book, to achieve what many much more ambitious treatises fail to do: namely, to set recent philosophical developments in their proper perspective. At first glance modern philosophical advances seem to be hopelessly destructive of earlier work. The truth of the matter is that they are only a more determined effort by philosophers to state their problems more explicitly. Their discussions tend inevitably towards the linguistic for a perfectly definite reason. We used to ask ourselves, when confronted by any particular proposition, whether that statement was true or false. Nowadays we realize that there is a prior question which we *must* ask: namely, whether the statement has any significance at all. Many pretentious philosophical bubbles go out bang when pricked by this analytical needle.

Mr. Hawton's treatment has another quality. It succeeds in giving us the feeling that philosophical problems, like scientific ones, are as urgent and interesting now as they were at man's first intellectual awakening in Ancient Greece. They have not been settled for all time, as traditionalists suppose. To those prospective readers who seek from philosophy final answers to all their questionings, I say in all seriousness that this book is *not* for them. For it presents philosophy as possessing perennial youth just because it is not finalistic. It is one of the ways in which a man shows that he is grown-up: the way of constant criticism. Philosophy is a disturber of intellectual peace, not a sedative.

CHAPTER ONE

What Philosophy is About

IN the sixth century B.C. something stirred into life on the cosmopolitan coast of Asia Minor that has had a profound significance for civilization. Men began to ask questions that had never been asked before. They began to ask what the world was made of and how it originated.

As far as our records show, this kind of speculation was without precedent. Both the Egyptians and the Babylonians had studied mathematics, astronomy, and medicine. They had made surprising progress in these subjects, although the results were expressed in an occult terminology. But such subjects had been hitherto studied by priests in sacred colleges. They had to be fitted into the framework of a religious cosmology. For laymen to venture an opinion on these deep matters was an innovation.

There is no evidence that the priestly caste ever debated the question of how the world came into existence. It would scarcely have occurred to them that the problem might be solved by the use of reason. They were satisfied that they knew the answers. They were guardians and interpreters of a sacred canon.

The discovery that the origin and meaning of life were questions that might be solved by rational discussion constitutes a landmark in human history. Only a very few individuals were conscious of it ; for the masses in those turbulent times life went on exactly as before. Nevertheless, the first blow for liberation had been struck. Man had begun to ask those questions which not only enriched his own consciousness, but ultimately led to control over the forces of nature.

The search started, not merely for information, but for

understanding. "Much learning does not bring understanding," said Heraclitus. And by understanding he meant,
"Nothing else but the exposition of the way in which the
universe works." Knowledge of this kind could not be derived
from traditional beliefs, as most people supposed. "One
must not act and talk like those reared with the narrow outlook, ' As it has been handed down to us.' "

Thus a rent was made in the blanket of superstition that had
hitherto stifled free inquiry. A new wind was blowing across
the world. Men were beginning to look at the world with new
eyes. They discovered problems that seemed capable of solution by this new and exciting method, by observing and reasoning. Before long this pursuit of wisdom was exalted into the
highest possible activity; and those who used the new,
intellectual instrument were called "lovers of wisdom"—
philosophers.

Naturally, the Ionians made no distinction between
philosophy and science. How recent such a separation is may
be seen by the fact that we still have chairs of natural philosophy
and mental philosophy in some of our universities, though the
subjects taught are, of course, physics and psychology. In
practice, however, philosophy now has a very restricted meaning. It has been the victim of its own success. Starting as an
inquiry into the working of the universe, as soon as some
branch of the investigation yielded positive results, that field
was removed from philosophy and given the name of a special
science.

Science is thus the offspring of philosophy; but so far from
devouring its parent, as it becomes more mature science turns
again to philosophy for guidance. Hence we find that physics,
the most advanced of the sciences, is becoming increasingly
philosophical. But even if every question about the working
of the universe could be appropriated by a particular science,
there would still be the question of how science itself works.
It has been suggested that science interrogating itself, fashion-
ing a science of science, may well be the last province left to
philosophy. But the prospect is merely an academic possi-

bility, because we are never likely to reach finality. The philosopher can be assured of a place as the critic of concepts, though he may have to give up constructing world systems.

It is impossible to give a satisfactory definition of philosophy unless a date is affixed to it. The reason for this is that the tasks undertaken by philosophers have differed in successive periods of historical development. No modern philosopher would have the temerity to tackle the problems that his counterpart in ancient Greece tried to solve. If we regard the most valuable part of the Greek contribution as the discovery of Reason as a new instrument, we can make a convenient division into ancient and modern philosophy, with the line of demarcation appearing when the instrument itself began to be critically examined.

There is an inevitable arbitrariness about all such classifications; but some point of departure must be taken, and there was clearly a very great change in the intellectual atmosphere of Europe in the sixteenth century. Once again new questions began to be asked. Once again a new wind was blowing, and great gaps appeared in the traditional picture of the universe. And once again this revolution of ideas took place outside the sacred colleges, and was largely the work of laymen.

During the Middle Ages speculation was practically confined to the monasteries. The trail blazed by the early Ionian Materialists had not been followed. The searchlight of inquiry had been diverted from a free exploration of the universe, and for that Plato must bear some of the blame. The logical tool that Plato and Aristotle had sharpened was used by the Scholastics to give an appearance of sweet reasonableness to their utterly preposterous theological beliefs. Unfortunately it was believed that nearly everything that could be found out about the universe was known. It merely remained to deduce the consequences.

It had been a tremendous leap forward when the Greeks discovered that some problems could be solved by intelligent discussion. The Scholastics, however, blocked any further advance by remaining content with *mere* discussion—by using logical arguments, as Galileo protested, " like magical incantations to charm the new planets out of the sky." It was argued, for example, that a heavy substance, such as lead, must fall to the ground at a faster rate than a lighter substance, such as feathers. As everyone knows, Galileo put the matter to the test.

By appealing to experiment Galileo started a new line of inquiry. Experiments had indeed been made in the classical world, but they had been virtually forgotten. Galileo began the division between experimental and speculative philosophy which issued in modern science. Almost at a stroke, philosophy seemed to lose half its kingdom; but we must remember that it had sought to embrace the whole universe, visible and invisible.

Modern philosophy really dates from this severance. No longer required to show the way in which the visible universe worked, it was driven to search for other riddles. It did not have to look far. The problems of the visible universe were left to Galileo, Kepler, Newton, and their successors; philosophers looked inside themselves, at their own minds. In doing so they were picking up the thread spun nearly 2,000 years earlier at Ephesus, when Heraclitus declared, " I searched *myself*."

Thus Descartes asked what knowledge a man possessed with unshakeable certitude, and he made his famous reply—*Cogito, ergo sum* : I think, therefore I am.

Bold innovator though he was in some respects, Descartes could not disentangle himself from medievalism. Both he and Leibniz asked their questions under the watchful eye of the theologian, and they had to make room in their systems for the existence of God and the immortality of the soul.

Locke is in some ways a more truly representative pioneer of what may be called modern philosophy. Locke asked questions that are still pertinent. Locke's questions led to Berkeley's, and such a vigorous opponent as Lenin has expressed the opinion—endorsed by Bertrand Russell—that no really new defence of the theory of Subjective Idealism has improved on the arguments of Berkeley.

Berkeley's views gave rise to the scepticism of Hume, who is still such a living force that he is the acknowledged inspiration of the most recent school of philosophy, Logical Positivism. Hume's scepticism so disturbed Kant that a very great deal of Kant's philosophy is an attempt to answer it. After Kant came Hegel, who attempted to answer everyone's questions at once by claiming to frame a universal philosophy which embraced all that had gone before it. But Hegel was not the end ; the most vigorous offshoot of Hegel was Dialectical Materialism, the official philosophy of the Soviet Union. This brings us right into the contemporary world—and still the philosophers are finding new questions to ask.

How Philosophy Progresses

Philosophy is unique in that its progress can be measured by the kind of questions it asks rather than by the success of its answers. It would be an over-statement to say that the answers do not greatly matter, but obviously they lack the immediate importance of the answers of the scientist. If we look merely at the answers we are confronted by a bewildering variety of theories, and with so little common agreement that the whole subject may seem a futile waste of time. Many histories of philosophy set these theories side by side, like so many wares on a shop counter, and the student may be excused for feeling " you pay your money and takes your choice."

Such an approach is, I am convinced, profoundly misleading. It is quite wrong to suppose that a history of philosophy resembles a vast Brains Trust, and that the student must sit back and listen to the opinions of Plato, Descartes, Locke, Kant, and so on, just as though they were being enunciated for the first time and could be judged on their individual merits. This is not history at all, for it leaves out of consideration the passage of time and the change of circumstances.

Philosophers do not live in a timeless vacuum. They see their problems in the perspective of the age to which they belong. The philosophers of the past, no matter how brilliant their intellects, were limited by the knowledge and vocabulary available. What would be the use of discussing infinity with Zeno if he had to remain ignorant of the mathematics which has solved the paradoxes he propounded ? Or, for that matter, how could we usefully discuss absolute space and time with Kant, if no reference could be made to relativity physics ?

It is something of an affectation for a modern man to call himself a Platonist or an Aristotelian. The answers that Plato and Aristotle gave may have been the best possible in their day, but the experience that has since accumulated cannot be ignored. We cannot fail to find stimulating suggestions abounding in many of the philosophies of the past, but we must make very big reservations. The most profitable course is surely to note how each philosopher, from Thales onwards, propounded some new question, found some fresh twist in argument ; and then we can follow the fortunes of the original idea as it is passed down the ages, like a ball, from inquirer to inquirer.

This means that to-day we have a great advantage. We can tap the experience of centuries. We not only know, for example, what Locke asked, but what Berkeley thought of it, what became of the question when it passed through the furnace of subsequent minds, such as Hume's and Kant's. It is purged of much dross in this historical process. There are flaws in many of the arguments that we would not have noticed ourselves, but which, in the course of time, have been revealed.

Looking very far back, we can also see—what was by no means evident at the time—that philosophy emerged from a background of religion. Just as religion itself, when it emerged from animistic magic, retained some of the conceptions of the lower level, so philosophy retained certain religious conceptions. It was some time before the cutting-power of Reason was properly appreciated. The instinct of the early philosophers was to set up a system as dogmatic, in its way, as a religious cosmology. As Professor Cornford writes : " The charm of the early Greek philosophers lies in the fact that, to a large extent, they did not trouble to invent bad arguments at all, but simply stated their beliefs dogmatically. They produced a system as an artist produces a work of art. Their attitude was, ' That is how the world is to be ' ; and the system itself, as distinct from any arguments that may be constructed to buttress the fabric, is thrown out, like a statue or a poem, as the expression of some thought or emotion that lies within and will have utterance." (*From Religion to Philosophy*.)

This oracular method was pursued by many great philosophers. They constructed vast and complicated systems which not only rivalled the religious accounts but made the science of the day seem very piecemeal and humdrum in comparison. These systems were claimed to be deductions from principles that were supposed to be self-evident. Consequently they seemed to offer a royal road to knowledge quite independent of the trial-and-error methods of science. They now litter the historical route of philosophical inquiry like the bones of extinct mammoths, and it seems improbable that we shall see many more such attempts.

This kind of philosophy is sometimes called " Metaphysics," and it was doomed when science took over the study of the working of the universe. The test of time has shown that it could not hope to compete with the experimental method. The study of nature cannot be carried out from an armchair. Nevertheless there are highly important studies that undoubtedly can be conducted from an armchair. Mathematics is one of them ; philosophy, as it is widely understood to-day, is another.

The Modern Problem

How is philosophy generally understood to-day ? What shift of meaning has occurred in our use of the word ? To answer this question adequately we must trace the adventures through history of those ideas thrown out by past philosophers. We shall see, I think, that progress has been made, albeit of an unusual and unexpected kind. We shall see that the principal gain has been framing clearer and more subtle questions and so increasing our understanding of what we are actually doing.

Subtle as the questions are, the subject-matter is close at

B

hand. We need not leave our armchairs to study it. We need not make philosophy our profession. Some of its finest achievements have been due to the brilliant amateur. It started its career as a series of speculations made by intelligent laymen in their spare time ; it was continued by slaves, soldiers, and statesmen, and at least as important work has been done by those who had some other means of livelihood—by doctors, opticians, schoolmasters, and civil servants—as by the professionals.

It would be absurd for an amateur to express an opinion on, say, the Quantum Theory ; but it is still possible for an amateur philosopher to say something of importance. Professional scientists often say very important things in their capacity as amateur philosophers ; but they often say foolish things, as Susan Stebbing showed in *Philosophy and the Physicists*. To defend the amateur philosopher does not mean that anybody can sit down at any moment and say something worth while about philosophy. Referring to Eddington, for example, Dr. Stebbing comments : " His lack of philosophical training (which I deduce from his writings, not from any private information as to his reading list) has made it possible for him to slip into pitfalls that he might otherwise have learnt to avoid."

Many who rush so eagerly into the fray have not troubled to consider how the questions that move them so deeply have been dealt with in the past. Without knowing it, they use arguments that were long ago exposed as fallacious, and they ask questions that have long been improved upon by careful amendments. To ignore the rich legacy of the past is surely presumptuous. The merchants of Miletus who pondered about the constitution of the universe several thousand years ago looked on much the same universe as we ourselves do ; their senses gave them the same data, their minds were at least as keen as the best modern minds. But they started with a blank page. There was no " reading list " to help them, not merely to solve their problems, but to re-state them in such a form that they were capable of solution.

Some of the problems which baffled philosophers in the past

have been partly, if not entirely solved. They have been taken over by the scientist. But the advance of science has disclosed fresh problems ; hence the spectacle of modern physicists turning their attention to philosophy instead of scorning it, as some of their predecessors were once tempted to do, because of the apparent paucity of results. They have turned to philosophy because it has now learnt to formulate more accurately questions that are of fundamental significance. When, in the seventeenth century, philosophy and science separated, the one turning to the analysis of experience, the other to physical experiment, the way was made clear for a new problem to take shape.

If anyone asks, therefore, what sort of questions philosophers are trying to answer to-day, a brief reply would be that they are mainly concerned with the terms in which we express what we experience. This should not be taken to imply that modern philosophy is necessarily subjective. Some, indeed, maintain that what we experience only exists in the mind ; others would deny it, though they might still be content to call what they analyse, Experience. The problem is to state what is meant by such terms as Experience, Mind, and Existing.

For Bertrand Russell, modern philosophy is neither metaphysical nor subjective. He writes : " It has been generally regarded as the business of philosophy to prove the great truths of religion. The new realism does not profess to be able to prove them, or even to disprove them. It aims only at clarifying the fundamental ideas of the sciences, and synthesizing the different sciences in a single comprehensive view of that fragment of the world that science has succeeded in exploring. It does not know what lies beyond ; it possesses no talisman for transforming ignorance into knowledge. It offers intellectual delights to those who value them, but it does not attempt to flatter human conceit as most philosophies do. If it is dry and technical, it lays the blame on the universe, which has chosen to work in a mathematical way rather than as poets or mystics might have desired." (*Sceptical Essays.*)

Whitehead has more sympathy with metaphysics, but he is opposed to the subjective view, although he is satisfied to speak of making an analysis in terms of Experience. " Speculative philosophy," he writes, " is the endeavour to frame a coherent, logical, necessary system of general ideas in terms of which every element of our experience can be interpreted." And to make this clearer, he continues : " Every science must devise its own instruments. The tool required for philosophy is language. Thus philosophy re-designs language in the same way that, in a physical science, pre-existing appliances are re-designed." (*Process and Reality.*)

It took many centuries of hard thinking before the realization dawned that words were not eternally fixed things, that they could be thrown on the scrap-heap and new words minted, that some apparently insoluble problems were due to difficulties of expression, that the accident of the grammatical form of a particular language itself created artificial problems that were unconnected with the subject under consideration. To-day the philosopher is confronted by his experiences—or, if you prefer to call it so, the Given—and he is free to make up any words he pleases, to invent whatever categories he finds convenient, in order to sort out these experiences and classify them. He himself, for example, makes the class which he calls Illusion ; and he makes another class which he calls Reality. There is no limit to the number of concepts he can construct—Matter, Mind, Life, Substance, Events, Cause, Law, etc.

But I am anticipating. The whole story cannot be told— yet. For the moment I merely wish to draw attention to an important difference between modern and ancient philosophy. That the modern attitude was latent in bygone controversies— Nominalism, for example—is, of course, true enough ; but the view that language is a tool for the interpretation of experience, and that the tool can be re-designed, is wholly new in its thorough-going application. Science, religion, literature, and even philosophy itself, must be expressed in language ; and so the criticism of language, because it is a criticism of the very instrument of thought, is fundamental.

" When *I* use a word," Humpty-Dumpty said in a rather

scornful tone, " it means just what I choose it to mean—neither more nor less."

" The question is," said Alice, " whether you *can* make words mean different things."

" The question is," said Humpty-Dumpty, " which is to be master—that's all ! "

Broadly speaking we can say that, for most ancient and medieval philosophers, words were the master ; and this is what one would expect to find in view of the historical emergence of philosophy from religion, with its quasi-magical attitude towards names. For most modern philosophers words are instruments, and although this attitude is held by widely divergent schools, it is one of the positive gains that have accrued from centuries of disputation.

To understand its importance, however, we must first study what has led up to it. No one, however gifted, can open a book by a contemporary philosopher and understand what he reads without any previous acquaintance with the history of philosophy. No one ignorant of the great controversies of the past could understand the simple quotations I have taken from Russell and Whitehead. The English is clear enough, but the dictionary meaning of the terms tells us nothing of their associations and the battles fought over them. For example, what is meant by Realism ? What is meant by Subjective, Objective, Coherent, Necessary, Interpretation ?

The Ionians would not have understood what was meant by re-designing language in order to interpret experience—devising a sort of net of abstract terms in which to fish among the chaos of the Given and arrange the catch in some kind of order. Nor can we ourselves understand what is meant by such a statement unless we know something of the process that the Ionians started and which gradually led up to the modern situation.

This book is primarily about modern philosophy. For reasons of space our consideration of the questions philosophers asked up to the seventeenth century must be brief. When, however, the problem of Knowledge is raised, I shall deal in more detail with that process of re-designing language which was unconscious to begin with, but which has now become the conscious and, indeed, the principal task left for the philosopher to perform.

Our journey will take us far back into history, and we shall follow the progress of ideas along their tortuous routes; we shall run into culs-de-sac and often have to retrace our steps; but all the time we shall be witnessing the most fascinating adventure of the human spirit as its consciousness deepens and it becomes aware of its own creative power. Such a journey, among the best thoughts of the best minds, is surely worth while if only for the intellectual delight it gives. It should help us to clarify our own ideas and think a little more correctly; and it should make us humble when we see how blind even great men can be, and tolerant as we realize what differing views of the universe it is possible to entertain.

Useful References

The Problems of Philosophy, by Bertrand Russell; 1912.
A History of Western Philosophy, by Bertrand Russell; 1947.
From Religion to Philosophy, by F. M. Cornford; 1912.
An Introduction to Logic, by H. W. B. Joseph; 1916.
A Sketch of Medieval Philosophy, by D. J. B. Hawkins; 1947.
The Open Society and Its Enemies (Vol I), by K. R. Popper; 1946.
The Grammar of Science, by Karl Pearson; 1911.
The Mind and Its Place in Nature, by C. D. Broad; 1925.
Science and Human Experience, by H. Dingle; 1931.
The Nature of the Physical World, by A. Eddington; 1928.
Language, Truth, and Logic, by A. J. Ayer; 1946.

CHAPTER TWO

The Discovery of Reason

THE downfall of Egypt, the rise of Persia, the struggle between the merchant class and the aristocratic landowner for control of the city-state, were the background against which the first philosophers asked the first questions. The great civilizations of the Nile and the Euphrates were conservative. Their science was practical rather than theoretical. It was concerned with civil engineering, irrigation, the construction of a correct calendar, and it was in the hands of priests who retained a mythical account of the origin of the universe. Greek religion was surprisingly free from the vices of ecclesiasticism. Neither Homer nor Hesiod took their gods too solemnly, and neither taught that the world had been made by the gods. On the contrary, as far back as the eighth century it was taught (by Hesiod) that Chaos produced the earth, which in turn produced the heavens; and everything else came from the mating of heaven and earth.

It was a small universe that these inquisitive Greeks contemplated. The stars were night's candles rather than suns; but they were not gods, as the Babylonians supposed. The stars were the progeny of the earth, and Anaximander (610–546 B.C.) seems to have pictured the earth gradually drying up by evaporation, man originally emerging as a fish-like creature from the sea. Here is the germ of an evolutionary theory the main interest of which is the early attempt to provide a *natural* account of origins.

Another point to notice is that all these Greeks were materialists. They had no conception of an immaterial God or an immaterial soul or immaterial forces. When they said that everything was ultimately water or mist or fire, they did not mean merely that the underlying substance was *like* water or mist or fire. When Empedocles (445 B.C.) said that the four primary elements were moved by two forces, Love and Hate, he was not merely speaking metaphorically. The forces of Empedocles were fluids. They were a kind of stuff, just as in primitive times even justice was regarded as a kind of stuff, the proper circulation of which caused the sun to shine and the crops to grow.

Our knowledge of the controversies that followed makes it difficult for us to imagine such unsophistication. But there were no such controversies for the Ionians to look back upon. All they had inherited was the magical theory of a mysterious *something*—a sort of mana—distributed unevenly throughout the objects of the universe. This mysterious something could not be seen with the eyes, so it was not a complete novelty for them to think of a reality behind the veil of appearances. The novelty was to investigate that reality by means of reason.

What is the world made of? they asked. What is the stuff of which everything we see is composed? Why do things have different shapes and colours, and why do they move about? Anaximander decided that there could be only one kind of substance, and everything in the world was some state of it. He called this substance the Indeterminate (or the Unlimited). It existed from all eternity, it was infinite in extent, and it was endowed with motion. This raw material could not be perceived by the senses, but it could be apprehended by Mind.

For our present purposes we need not go into the details of these early guesses. It is sufficient to note the important ideas that were thrown off almost as by-products of the game of speculation. But the belief in a unity behind the shifting variety of appearances, and the conviction that reason could discover a deeper truth than the senses, were of the highest importance.

The Problem of Change

The point was taken up and given even sharper emphasis by Heraclitus (504 B.C.). He boldly opposed the evidence of reason to the evidence of the senses. The eyes and ears, he said, were bad witnesses ; the mind must interpret their evidence, and wisdom lay in the interpretation. Wisdom—or, as we should say, Truth—did not consist in mere observation. It consisted in using the reason to perceive the unity beneath the diversity which otherwise baffled the senses. Wherever you look you see changes taking place. " Everything is in Flux and nothing is at rest." Again, in a famous phrase, " You cannot step twice into the same river."

Thus the question posited by Thales and Anaximander takes a new turn with Heraclitus. He accepts their belief that reason can find an underlying unity in the world, but he asks how this unity can be reconciled with the fact of change ? He asks a question to which a wholly satisfactory answer has yet to be found, and in our own time the philosopher mainly preoccupied with it has been Bergson. The answer which Heraclitus gave inspired the stupendous system of Hegel. Unfortunately we have only a few fragments of the book which he deposited in the temple at Ephesus, where he was, by birth, heir to the priest-kingship.

The fact of change makes it difficult to describe the behaviour of the mysterious substance underlying appearances as though it were composed of inert lumps of stuff. For whenever change occurs—and it is always occurring—something becomes different and yet something must remain the same. So the stuff of the world, according to Heraclitus, is not water ; it is fire.

Indeed, material bodies *are* a sort of fire, waxing and waning, flaring up and dying down according to law. " The sun will not overstep the measure of his path ; but if he does, then the goddesses of Fate, the handmaids of Justice, will know how to find him. . . . The order of the world, which is the same for all things, has not been made, neither by a god nor a man. It always was, is, and will be, an eternally living fire, with a law that measures its flaring up and a law that measures its dying down."

To translate this picturesque language into modern speech is scarcely possible without covertly adding to it. But here, in embryo, is the very fundamental idea that the world must be interpreted in terms of processes and not of things. The apparent stability which makes us mistake processes for things is like the apparent stability of a flame in a windless place when it looks solid. Heraclitus explained this stability as a kind of balance achieved by opposite forces within the same process. This internal tension, due to warring elements, is the source of their development. " All things develop through strife and necessity."

The question " What is the world made of ? " had led on quite naturally to the question " How does the world change ? " In the course of the transition there was a great deal of fanciful speculation that only interests the historian now, but apart from the detailed answers there were a number of exceedingly fruitful ideas that added to the intellectual armoury. The essential ideas that emerged were : (a) That the world is governed by necessity (law). (b) That its laws can be discovered by the human mind. (c) That the world, including gods and souls, is composed of one substance, despite appearances to the contrary, which exists in space and time (i.e., it is material). (d) That the unity perceived by reason presents a public world for the philosopher in contrast to the private world of un-enlightened individuals : " Those who are awake have one common world ; those who are asleep turn to their private worlds " (Heraclitus). (e) That the world is the totality of changing processes, and its stabilities result from the union of opposites.

This was a remarkable achievement for the sixth century B.C. No doubt the violence and instability of the times helped to fashion some of the new concepts. The rapidity of social change brought the abstract problem of change to the forefront. About the same period as these questions were being asked on the coast of Asia Minor, similar discussions were taking place in the Greek colonies founded in Italy and Sicily, whither political refugees, exiles, and displaced persons had fled from the menace of Persia.

Mysticism and Mathematics

Pythagoras of Croton (571–497 B.C.) formed a community whose mystical and political aspirations do not concern us here. He also asked what the world was made of and how reason could discover the answer. He offered a very curious solution. He said in effect that the world was made of numbers, and that the answers could be found by studying mathematics.

The modern mind thinks of numbers as abstractions. To say that the world is made of numbers seems as outrageous as saying that it is composed of words. Pythagoras, however, thought of numbers as we think of material things. They were bits of stuff; and points with magnitude, lines with thickness were the ultimate furniture of the universe.

The practical significance of his number-mysticism was the impetus it gave to the study of mathematics. The suggestion that wisdom—i.e., the truth about the working of the world— was largely mathematical was a tremendous step forward. The belief that mathematics can show us how the mind of God works fascinated some of the subtlest intellects for thousands of years after—one is reminded of Sir James Jeans's dictum that the universe is a thought in the mind of the great Mathematician.

The Pythagoreans knew that the pitch of a taut string varied exactly with the length, and they decided that the heavenly bodies must obey a similar law—that their varying distances caused them to emit different sounds as they revolved, and that the whole of these sounds taken together was like a sublime orchestra, governed by mathematical law. The Ionians used their eyes, so to speak, where the Pythagoreans used their ears. To them the world was not so much like water, or mist, or fire, as like sound. It was like a harmony of vibrations, the music of the spheres.

Unfortunately the real world could not be fitted to the Procrustean bed of the mathematics of the time. For example, the ratio of the diagonal of a square to the side could not be expressed as a whole number, and the scandal of irrational numbers in a rational universe was so great that the discovery of incommensurability is said to have been hushed up.

Pythagoras failed in his solution, but he succeeded in calling attention to the importance of mathematics as a clue to the structure of the world. And after Pythagoras the ball fell to Parmenides of Elea (504 B.C.), who was a contemporary of Heraclitus, to whose central problem he offered an original and paradoxical solution. He went much farther than Heraclitus in opposing reason to the senses.

Heraclitus had said that everything was constantly changing. Parmenides retorted that, on the contrary, it could be proved by reason that nothing could possibly change. If the senses brought evidence to the contrary they were deceptive. Change was an illusion, because whatever is, is ; and whatever is not, is not. It follows that whatever changes both is and is not, simultaneously. This seemed an intolerable contradiction. How, therefore, can we believe in change and yet remain true to reason ? This gave rise to the argument that change must mean the appearance of something new ; but for something new, something that did not exist before, to come into existence, entails that something is created out of nothing, which again is unthinkable. So, however ridiculous it may seem to deny the reality of change, there can be no logical escape.

To-day the problem of how something quite new can arise is central for Emergent Evolutionists and Dialectical Materialists. By declaring that the emergence of novelty was logically impossible, the Eleatics raised another, equally important question —to what extent can pure logic give us information about the world ? Since those days opinion has been deeply divided on the point ; those who trusted to logic, come what may, were Rationalists, in the strict sense of the word, and they constructed elaborate systems of metaphysics ; their great rivals were the Empiricists, who put their trust in experience.

One of the most troublesome of all philosophical problems has been the relation between the verdict of logic and experience. By standing on his head so dramatically, and declaring that everyone else was the victim of an illusion, Parmenides called sharp attention to the problem, though obviously he did not solve it. No one outside a lunatic asylum could consistently deny the fact of change.

Materialism and Idealism

Parmenides opened the door for the metaphysicians just as Pythagoras opened the door for the mathematicians. Then came Leucippus and Democritus, in the second half of the fifth century, with a theory that opened the door for all subsequent physics—the atomic theory.

Once again, What was the world made of? Atoms, said Leucippus; small particles of matter separated from one another by void. The mysterious something underlying appearances was an infinite number of atoms. They were as impenetrable and changeless in their composition as the One of Parmenides; they were One. They differed merely in form and arrangement. All the changes perceived by the senses were due to the regroupings of these primary atoms.

The details of this brilliant guess were supplied by Democritus of Abdera (c. 420 B.C.). The work of his predecessors suddenly seemed like blind groping in the face of a solution that appeared satisfying both to reason and common sense alike.

The universe was composed of indivisible atoms and void; their movements and patterns were due to necessity. Yet, we are impelled to ask, what is meant by necessity? What ensures the orderly arrangement of the atoms? What place can be found in a world of blind, material atoms for the Reason (the mind) which has discovered this reality hidden behind the veil of the sensuous world? How can thoughts be the *same* as the movements of material particles?

The search for the ultimate stuff of which the world was made was bound to raise questions about the search and the searchers; for in a way both seem to lie outside the process studied. But it was too early for the problem of knowledge, as it appears to modern philosophers, to emerge. What was inevitable, however, was for someone to try to define more accurately the relation between the surprising and paradoxical world disclosed by logic and the common-sense world which seemed so very different.

The original statement of Hesiod, that in the beginning was Chaos, and Chaos produced the earth, was in effect re-written by Anaxagoras (500–428 B.C.) as follows : " In the beginning all things were in confusion, then Mind came and reduced them to order." This was regarded as a cosmic operation. The Mind referred to is not the mind of the philosopher. It would have been impossible at that date to re-write it as a modern subjectivist might do : " Primary experience is a chaos, but *my* mind reduces it to order."

To begin with, Idealism was objective. The question which gave rise to the philosophical theory called Idealism is this : " Is the material universe the result of mind or does it give birth to mind in the course of its development ? " Now in classical times Mind could only mean God ; the idea of treating one's own mind as though one were God, creating the world out of a chaos of experience, is essentially modern—at least in Western philosophy.

The Problem of Universals

The seeds of Objective Idealism are found in Pythagoras and Parmenides, but it is in Plato (427–348 B.C.) that they come to fruition. The pre-Socratics were mostly materialistic, though not quite in the modern sense. They made no sharp distinction between living and dead matter ; but the soul was regarded as a material object.

With Plato the inquiry into the mysterious reality behind the scenes raises the question of immaterial being, quite apart even from souls and gods. Just as Pythagoras regarded numbers as things, so Plato regarded abstract ideas as existing in timeless independence of the material world.

Plato made no attempt to work out a detailed metaphysical system. Indeed, we must not look to the Greeks for such systems. They were explorers rather than builders ; they were discoverers of ideas, and it is largely with the bricks that they supplied that subsequent systems were built.   No summary of the philosophies of Plato and Aristotle can be made here ; all I wish to do is to call attention to the most outstanding additions made to mankind's intellectual equipment.

There are many disputes about what Plato actually meant. All that interests us now is what he seemed to mean to others, what new problems his theories stimulated.   By Plato's time attention was focused on the remarkable fact that the world of common-sense objects seemed utterly different from the picture that logic had painted.

No one could hear the music of the spheres ; no one could see the atoms of Democritus.   Must it, then, be supposed that the whole adventure of the mind was a mistake ?   Which was the illusion—the world disclosed by logic or the world perceived by the senses ?   Plato answered without hesitation that the world of logic was real.   It must be accepted whatever the affront to common-sense.

He analysed common-sense beliefs.   Everyone must admit that some things were very beautiful, and others less so ; some actions were just, and others unjust in varying degrees.   This could only be the case if some things contained beauty, and some acts had a certain amount of justice.   If there were degrees of beauty and degrees of justice, there must be a Beauty and a Justice that were perfect, absolute.

To say that these terms are general is merely to say that they are not confined to a particular case, but are spread over a multitude of particular cases.   So we have particular facts, on the one hand ; and general or universal facts, on the other. No amount of examination of the particular will give us the universal.   Beautiful things exhibit beauty, but they must all fall short of beauty itself.

Now Plato applied this ingenious analysis to all abstract terms.   The gold coin you hold in your hand is—what ?   To describe it you have to say it is yellow and circular, etc.   You can only describe it in terms of universals—yellowness and circularity.   There is no escape.   Every particular is com-pounded of universals.   These universals must therefore be

real.   They must exist.   Beauty, yellowness, circularity must
exist.   They define gold.

Look again at the gold coin.   Try to think away these universals.   Subtract colour, shape, size, weight—what is left in
the end ?   Only the bare substance that passively underlies all
things—bare matter stripped of attributes, and which waits
patiently to receive definition.

This must not be taken as a summary of Plato's actual arguments.   It is the train of thought he inevitably started and
which ultimately led to such conundrums as, What is the
difference between mere Being (without any qualities) and
Nothing ?   Is a particular thing (a gold coin) composed of a
substratum plus attributes, substance plus accidents ;   or is it
just the sum-total of its appearances ?

Democritus tried to reduce the world to two elements, Atoms
and Void.   Plato tried to reduce it to Matter and Form.
What is unique about the Platonic solution is that the forms
were believed to exist independently.   The everyday world
revealed matter stamped with form ;   but the forms are only
imperfectly shown.   Behind the scenes, beyond time and
space, there is another world ;   it is perfect, exact, and delightful.   There the soul can contemplate pure beauty, pure justice
—the whole procession of universals can be seen in their
sublime perfection.

Knowledge of reality is not given by the senses but is perceived with the eyes of the soul, whose proper object is the
study of forms or universal ideas.   Science is therefore independent of experience—a most dangerous idea, as it turned
out, though the practical merit of Platonism was that by
emphasizing, as did Heraclitus, the uselessness of mere unrelated bits of information it focused attention on the search for
logical and mathematical relationships.

Whitehead puts it :   " The safe general characterization of
the European philosophical tradition is that it consists of a
series of footnotes to Plato.   I do not mean the systematic
scheme of thought which scholars have doubtfully extracted
from his writings.   I allude to the wealth of general ideas

scattered through them. His personal endowments, his wide opportunities for experience at a great period of civilization, his inheritance of an intellectual tradition not yet stiffened by excessive systematization, have made his writings an inexhaustible mine of suggestion." (*Process and Reality*.)

The Foundations of Logic

The brilliant and wayward genius of Plato, so intoxicating to poets and mathematicians, was corrected on its more mystical course by the sobriety of Aristotle (384–322 B.C.). Plato had raised the problem of universals. Aristotle took it over ; but he could not admit that they had any separate existence. For Aristotle the actual universe lay between the two extremes of formless matter and matterless form (God).

Plato's enthusiasm for mathematics had pointed the way to the physicist ; Aristotle's gift for classification pointed the way to the biologist. Looking back on two centuries of achievement, he asked a most fundamental question. Granted that the world is composed of some primary substance endowed with general qualities, and that it is in the process of development, what makes it move ? What is the *cause* ?

For long afterwards the task for the scientist seemed to be mainly to classify phenomena and to search for causes. Aristotle classified Cause itself into four types—Material, Formal, Efficient, Final. He recognized very clearly the extreme complexity of Cause. Everything that happened must have a cause ; every cause must have an effect. Moreover, effects must bear some resemblance to their causes. Here was material for the famous controversy of Freewill versus Determinism, already implicit in the atomic theory. Here, too, was food for the medieval theologians ; for if everything had a cause, surely there must be a First Cause ?

Aristotle insisted that there must be a purpose in things ; they moved as they did in pursuance of some final aim. The notion of a final cause and the self-adaptation of evolving organisms towards some ultimate goal still lurks even in the outlook of scientists who would indignantly deny it, and under-

C

lies the popular query : " What is the meaning of Life ? What is the purpose of the Universe ? " The vitalism of Driesch is modern Aristotelianism.

Two other most useful concepts were added by Aristotle— Potentiality and Actuality. The oak-tree is not created out of nothing ; the sort of change from acorn to oak exists potentially in the acorn. Matter, stripped of its qualities, is therefore awaiting passage from the potential to the actual.

Aristotle classified the working of reason, and thus founded the science of formal logic. He made the basis of it the simplest kind of proposition, a subject with a predicate : " All men are mortal " or " The Rose is red."

He demonstrated how it was possible to argue from the first proposition that all men are mortal : Socrates is a man ; therefore Socrates is mortal. And why it was wrong to say, for example, " The rose is red ; the poppy is red ; therefore a rose is a poppy." He supplied the rules with which fallacies in this type of argument—a conclusion drawn from two premises—could be detected.

No more could be expected of him. His powerful mind ranged over all that was known of natural science, philosophy, æsthetics, ethics, and politics. The depth and comprehensiveness of his thought remain one of the wonders of the world. Between them, Plato and Aristotle made the intellectual mould in which all speculation took shape for more than a thousand years.

That the medieval Church wrought a dogma out of his philosophy was no fault of Aristotle. He could scarcely have foreseen that the doctrine of substance and accidents would be used to explain Transubstantiation, and be made virtually binding on the faithful.

The limitations of Aristotelian logic have only begun to be fully realized. One weakness is that it suggests an invisible, qualityless substratum : even a simple statement, " The rose is red," smuggles in an independent entity, to which the quality of redness can be added. Modern philosophy, quite early in its career, questioned the necessity for postulating such an underlying substance.

We shall return to this topic in later chapters, but for the moment it is sufficient to point out that when the contemporary physicist speaks of events and processes, instead of things, when space and time are regarded as relations between events, a sharp break is made with one of the most fundamental assumptions of classical philosophy. When people complain that contemporary science outrages common-sense they usually mean that it outrages Aristotle—and they forget how far Aristotle himself had travelled from those common-sense conceptions which most ancient philosophers were united in despising as " delusive opinion."

The questions which were asked in the millennium that followed Plato and Aristotle seem to the modern ear to be futile quibbling and word-spinning. They were mainly concerned with the status of universals. There were, no doubt, excellent political and economic reasons why science could not yet develop. There were also very good intellectual reasons why scientific theory was paralysed. It was largely held up because the wrong sort of questions were asked.

Instead of asking *how* moving objects actually behaved, men asked : " *What* is motion ? " and so on. They mistook the study of verbal definitions for the study of actual phenomena. They looked for mysterious " essences "—which was as vain as the search for Platonic forms or the philosophers' stone.

Philosophy would have foundered in a morass of sterile word-spinning if it had not been given a fresh orientation. Its progress depends on the insight with which old problems are given a new formulation. The answers do not give us the final truth we thirst for, but they stimulate us to frame more and more cogent questions.

If anyone supposes that I am suggesting that the latest theory to appear is necessarily an improvement on any earlier theory, he has misread what I have tried to state very plainly. Theories themselves do not necessarily improve as time moves on, but our experience obviously becomes wider and the old formulations can no longer cover the whole of it. We find fresh turnings in the intellectual labyrinth ; we do not find the way out, but our knowledge of the maze in which we wander is nevertheless increased.

Useful References

Greek Thinkers, by J. Gomperz, Eng. trs.; 1901.
Outlines of Greek Philosophy, by E. Zeller, 13th ed.; 1931.
Thales to Plato, by J. Burnet; 1914.
Plato and His Contemporaries, by G. C. Field; 1930.
Plato's Theory of Knowledge, by F. M. Cornford; 1935.
An Introduction to Ancient Philosophy, by A. H. Armstrong; 1947.
Aristotle, by W. Jaeger, Eng. trs.; 1934.
Stoic and Epicurean, by R. D. Hicks; 1910.

There are many good translations of Plato and Aristotle. F. M. Cornford's translation of *Timæus* (1937) and *The Republic* (1941) have valuable explanatory notes. Jowett's translation of the Dialogues (5 vols.) was re-issued in 1925. The Oxford translation of Aristotle (ed. J. A. Smith and W. D. Ross) is complete in 11 volumes. Munro's translation of Lucretius was published with text commentary and an introduction by Prof. Andrade in 1928. For neo-Platonists see *The Enneads of Plotinus*, translated by Mackenna and Page (1926–1930), and *Select Passages Illustrative of Neoplatonism*, by E. R. Dodds (1923).

CHAPTER THREE

The Rape of Reason

THE profound social changes in the sixteenth and seventeenth centuries were reflected in a new world outlook. The earth had become vaster. The Mediterranean no longer seemed the centre of civilization. Italy had lost its importance, America had been discovered and India was being opened up. The struggle for material power underlay a religious conflict—now between Catholics and Protestants, and now between rival Protestant sects themselves.

It is a mistake, however, to suppose that the break with the medieval outlook was sharp and abrupt. Looking back at those distant ideological conflicts, we can see how much both Catholics and Protestants had in common. The philosopher had to be just as careful to avoid offending the one as the other. New questions were being asked, new formulations of very old problems, but quite often the answers remained in note-books or in manuscripts that the authors dared not publish. Quite often, as in Greece, the philosophers went into voluntary exile. Galileo was placed under house-arrest, and the nervous Hobbes spent many years out of England. Spinoza was excommunicated and once stoned by an angry mob, and his *Ethics* was not published in his lifetime. Leibniz's *Nouveaux Essais*, the best exposition of his philosophy, was not published until fifty years after his death, and his important notes were only published comparatively recently.

Philosophy often had the air of a conspiracy. It fell, in some cases deservedly, under the suspicion of being subversive of the established order of things. This, indeed, was not new. Socrates had been judicially murdered. The Pythagoreans and Epicureans were severely persecuted. Abélard, Roger Bacon, and Bruno were variously punished. The popular charge was usually " atheism," and although it was little more than a term of abuse, in self-defence philosophers were obliged to take great pains to disprove it.

Perhaps this was one reason why so many of them have been preoccupied with demonstrating the existence of God. The search for proofs of God's existence did not end with the Middle Ages. Descartes, Leibniz, Spinoza, Locke, and Berkeley, all tried their hands at it. Another very powerful motive, it is to be feared, was that God could be invoked whenever a gap in a rational explanation had to be patched up. Descartes and Leibniz quite shamelessly employed a dialectical *deus ex machina*.

In examining their philosophies, therefore, we must remember the limitations imposed by the age in which they lived. Protest against their predecessors as they might, they saw the world through spectacles fashioned by the Greeks. What brings them closer to ourselves was their growing awareness of this very fact—that the world seen through the spectacles of Greek rationalism looked utterly unlike the world they saw when they removed those spectacles.

With their naked eyes they saw a small sun climbing across the sky ; they were aware of everyday objects with colours, smells, and noises, objects that changed shape, grew, decayed, and seemed to disappear. How was it possible to believe that the earth moved and the sun was stationary when the evidence of the senses was utterly to the contrary ?

But looked at through the spectacles of a philosopher the ordinary world vanished and a wholly different picture was seen. Admittedly the picture varied, according to whose glasses you borrowed, but in any case it seemed to bear no resemblance to the world seen with the naked eyes. So there seemed to be two worlds—the one disclosed by reason, the other by common-sense. And it was inevitable that men should continue to ask how these two pictures were related ? How far should they trust the evidence of reason when it seemed to contradict the plain evidence of their senses ?

The Deception of the Senses

This question was raised afresh by Galileo (1564–1642). He answered emphatically in favour of the world disclosed by reason. He was the pioneer of experimental philosophy, but the impression that he was the first of the philosophical empiricists—those who give priority to the world of sense-perception—is not quite correct. The full significance of the clash between the two worlds could hardly have been apparent in Galileo's time. Referring to the Copernican theory, he wrote : " I cannot sufficiently admire the eminence of those men's wits, that have received and held it to be true, and with the sprightliness of their judgements offered such violence to their own senses, as that they have been able to prefer that which their reason dictated to them to that which sensible experiments represented most manifestly to the contrary."

In other words, although we *seem* to see the sun move across the sky, the sun does not in fact move across the sky. Reason shows that the earth moves and the sun is stationary. Reason does such violence to the senses that he speaks of " the rape of reason on the senses." But we must trust reason, and not the senses. They can deceive us, but reason gives us the truth.

Our senses deceive us grossly by representing ordinary objects as coloured, noisy, tasty, and aromatic. In reality— i.e., according to reason—they do not possess colours, sound, tastes, or smells. These qualities are contributed by our senses and do not exist in the outside world. " But that external bodies, to excite in us these tastes, these odours, and these sounds, demand other than size, figure, number, and slow or rapid motion, I do not believe ; and I judge that, if the ears, the tongue, and the nostrils were taken away, the figure, the numbers, and the motions would indeed remain, but not the odours, nor the tastes, nor the sounds, which, without the living animal, I do not believe are anything else than names, just as tickling is precisely nothing but a name if the armpit and the nasal membrane be removed."

This sort of language has a ring of familiarity. The old

Scholastic controversies about *universalia ante rem* (Realism) *in re* (Aristotelianism) or *post rem* (Nominalism) mean little to us to-day. But we can well understand the argument that, in the phrase coined by Locke, there are primary and secondary qualities. We know quite well that there is no science of colours, sounds, tastes, and smells. To treat these facts of experience scientifically a way had to be devised of expressing them as quantities. Unless they could somehow be translated into quantities it did not seem possible to treat them mathematically. To Galileo the credit must largely be given of perceiving this necessity. Democritus had also argued in favour of primary and secondary qualities, but Galileo put the inquiry on a practical basis by showing how it was possible to frame laws by dealing with quantities.

Experience was not thereby neglected; it was classified. Part of it was isolated from the rest of reality and studied. Thus, for Galileo the field of study was matter in motion. To investigate this he did not merely meditate on the meaning of the word " motion," as though an improved definition would yield new information. He watched material objects actually moving. He dropped a one-pound weight together with a ten-pound weight and demonstrated to the astonished crowd that they struck the ground simultaneously. He used his small telescope and saw that the Milky Way was composed of separate stars, that Jupiter had satellites, that the moon had mountains.

Instead of making the easy answer that the planets were kept in motion by an unmoved Mover, he realized—forestalling Newton—that no external force was necessary to keep them moving in a straight line uniformly; what had to be explained was the cause of their deviations. Newton was born in the year that Galileo died (1642), and Newton led the way triumphantly along the trail that Galileo had blazed, giving the first exact definition of mass, and formulating a law that applied to all material bodies.

This development was known at the time as " natural " or " experimental " philosophy. Nowadays we call it " science," and although it seems a little hard on the philosophers, it is more convenient to restrict the name " philosophy " to those investigations which have not yielded such excellent results. But it cannot be too strongly stressed that experimental philosophy was not mainly concerned with collecting observed instances. Bacon over-emphasized this aspect. Knowledge, as Heraclitus had pointed out, is not just the amassing of information— " polymathy," as he rather contemptuously called it—but the rational correlation of evidence. Thus, although science arose out of an attempt to explain the behaviour of quite ordinary things that everyone could see, it could only furnish an explanation by inventing things that no one could possibly see. When Diogenes complained, of the Platonic Ideas, " I can see a table, but not tableness," he was striking at the root of the scientific method which Galileo did so much to devise. For who can see force or inertia or mass ?

Mind and Machine

The insistence on experiment and observation compelled the natural philosopher to keep his feet on the ground. In the last resort he had to account for " brute fact," and if he failed, the stately ship in which he set sail into such strange seas of thought must founder. But some distinction between universal forms and particulars, or between the world of reason and the world of sense-perception, had to be maintained. For centuries philosophers have struggled to reconcile the two within some single comprehensive system.

Physical science was amazingly successful within the isolated domain it had selected. Was it not possible to describe the whole of human experience in this manner ? Hobbes (1588–1679) thought so. Influenced by Galileo, he was deeply impressed by the enormous simplification of reducing the entire universe, animate and inanimate, to matter and motion. If everything that existed consisted of purely material particles, then all changes boiled down to changes in position, and were accordingly amenable to mathematical treatment. Why should not human beings and human societies be regarded as systems of mechanical motion ?

Descartes (1596–1650) was also stimulated by this somewhat startling view, and he accepted a good deal of it. Like so many of the great thinkers of his age, he was a mathematician, and he was anxious to apply mathematical reasoning as widely as possible. It seemed like a sheet-anchor, giving certainty and security, amid the shifts of mere opinion and guesswork. But to Descartes it seemed that Hobbes had thrown away the baby with the bath-water. The world of reason, the world of atoms moving in accordance with mathematical law, constituted, indeed, a reality behind appearances, but one thing was left out —the reasoner.

For present purposes we can neglect the purely personal problem which confronted Descartes as an orthodox Catholic. We will ignore the unpleasant fact that when he heard of the condemnation of Galileo he suppressed a book he was writing which accepted the Copernican hypothesis. His objection to the full doctrine of mechanical Materialism was unquestionably genuine, and in different ways the same objection had been expressed by many other philosophers. Granted that the world is material, and even a machine, how can we account for mind—reason—which studies this machine and discovers its laws ?

There is matter in motion, said Descartes ; but there is also something else—there is thought. If anything, it is easier to reduce matter to thought, than thought to matter. We can imagine, for example, what it would be like to lack the organs of sight, smell, touch, and hearing. We can imagine a state of affairs in which the whole of what we call the external world is no more than a dream. Everything we assert of the external world may be an interpretation of the elements of our consciousness, and a determined sceptic could cast doubt upon it. What the sceptic cannot doubt is the fact that someone is doubting, the fact that he himself is thinking.

Descartes was searching for a starting-point. In this he believed that he was applying the method of mathematics to philosophy. The mathematician begins with very simple and discrete notions, and from these he proceeds to make deductions. What simple notion could the philosophers start from ? What truth can he take as a basis which is utterly beyond dispute ? And so Descartes arrived at his famous *Cogito, ergo sum*—I think, therefore I am.

By thinking, he meant consciousness in general. What he was really saying was that the fact of consciousness, which was indubitable, implied a conscious subject. He felt that that was axiomatic, because he was expressing himself in the logical form clarified by Aristotle—a form of language so ingrained in European thought that it seemed to show forth the very texture of the universe. If he had met a Buddhist when he was in Amsterdam, he would probably have been very surprised indeed to discover that there were people to whom thinking did not seem to imply a permanent ego. But Descartes cast his experience in the subject-predicate mould. He inherited the Greek tradition with its belief in a mysterious " something," underlying phenomena, a subject which was qualified by adjectives.

Why should there be only *one* kind of substance ? Why not two, three, four, or even an infinite number of substances ? Indeed, on the Cartesian definition, there seems to be no reason whatever to restrict the universe to one kind of fundamental stuff. " When we perceive any attribute," he writes, " we therefore conclude that some existing thing or substance to which it may be attributed, is necessarily present." Attributes require a substance, just as a predicate requires a subject. But substance, in Descartes' famous phrase, " requires nothing but itself in order to exist."

Dualism

It is no exaggeration to say that most people are still Cartesians without knowing it. The popular, common-sense philosophy, based on the Christian tradition, separates man into body and soul. The body is composed of matter, which is ordinarily conceived of as tiny particles in motion. The soul is regarded as a separate substance ; accordingly it survives the loss of the body.

On a somewhat higher level of discussion, a distinction is still made between the concepts of psychology. We talk of mind *and* body. We consider a variety of theories as to how such totally dissimilar things can act on one another. It seems, on the face of it, quite impossible that a material substance should influence, or be influenced by, an immaterial substance. There are all kinds of theories—Parallelism, Epiphenomenalism, Instrumentalism, and so on—and in sheer despair the Behaviourists have been driven to deny the existence of consciousness, which was Descartes' fundamental postulate. Unless we adopt this extreme position, no matter what theories we hold in private, we seem to be compelled in practice to act as though mental concepts and material concepts were not capable of being translated into a common language. We may believe, or merely hope, that the psycho-analyst and the physiologist are really talking about the same thing in different words, but it is evident enough that they must still go on using different words. If it is true that every thought can be correlated with the movement of an atom in the brain, no one can yet do the trick.

Hence the extraordinary importance of the problem that Descartes formulated. His solution was a model of neatness and ingenuity. In brief, he said that two substances were required for any explanation of the world that included the author of the explanation. One substance was matter, which had the characteristic of extension. Three-dimensional matter in motion was all that was needed to account for the world of perception. The visible universe was a vast machine ; even animals were no more than pieces of clockwork. If it should be asked whether this external world really existed—and very soon, as we know, that question was to be raised—the answer was that God would not deceive man. It would be blasphemous to suppose that we were dupes of a Supreme Illusionist.

In addition to extended substance (matter), there was thinking substance (mind). The mind (*l'âme raisonnable*) was not a blank, which passively received impressions from without, as Locke subsequently taught ; on the contrary, it was internally supplied with a certain number of fixed ideas. With the help of these innate ideas—God, self, cause, motion, extension, etc. —the human reason could arrive at truth by reflection. It could also make mistakes, because an act of judgment involved the will. That such a mind should be able to modify matter, that the fluent world of thought and extension should go on existing from moment to moment, instead of being annihilated by the passage of time, were due to the action of God, whose existence could be proved by logic.

Now here, if we ignore the theology, is a mine of suggestion of extraordinary richness ; future philosophers were to dig into it deeply and to find, at every turn, that fresh possibilities were excited in their minds. By stating such a problem, and elaborating a method, Descartes started investigations that would have astonished him. Let us look more closely at some of the vistas opened up.

Deductive Rationalism

(1) *Method*. The most fundamental of Descartes' assumptions is that truths about the existent world can be discovered by reasoning only. This was the almost universal belief of his Age. He claimed to proceed by systematic doubt, yet it never occurred to him to doubt that logic could give genuine information about the world. The possibility that logic might be a closed system, that its conclusions were contained in its premises, that its axioms were tautologies, that the whole procedure of deduction from simple and distinct notions might be really an argument in a circle, did not very seriously disturb the confidence of philosophers until later.

A similar procedure, though it led to different results, was followed by Spinoza and Leibniz. This was the Golden Age of Rationalism—using the word in a strict, technical sense. Modern Rationalism is something quite different, and in some respects quite opposite, since it is closely identified with what the seventeenth-century thinkers called experimental philosophy.

The method of introspection, which Descartes used, although

not essentially novel, was original in its application. It was bound to lead to subjectivism. The argument that God was incapable of deceiving was too weak to save the objectivity of the external world.

(2) *Substance*. Descartes formulated his central problem in terms of substance and attribute. He decided, as we have seen, in favour of two substances. This naturally gave rise to dissatisfaction, especially as he had to invoke God to meet the difficulties inherent in such a view. Once an analysis has been made in terms of matter and mind, it is inevitable that someone should appeal to the maxim attributed (falsely) to William of Occam, which stated (1347)—*Entia praeter necessitatem non sunt multiplicanda* : Entities are not to be multiplied without necessity.

Do we need more than one substance ? Is that substance matter or mind ? Finally, can we not drop the notion of substance altogether, in the interest of logical economy ?

Struggling with these questions, philosophers have tried to express the whole of reality in the language of physics or psychology. We have had Monism, and Dualism, both of which result from the subject-predicate form of stating the problem.

(3) *Mechanism*. The view that the material world behaves throughout like a machine has been almost unquestioned, except in comparatively recent times, in orthodox scientific circles, and it is still a respectable though less fashionable theory. By distinguishing between primary and secondary qualities all phenomena are reduced to moving particles of matter—or even to pulses of energy—and so, it is claimed, all phenomena must obey laws which can be expressed mathematically. If we know what forces are acting on a particle we can surely predict its movement ; and if so, as Laplace suggested, a mind capable of knowing the disposition of every particle in the universe would be able to predict all future events.

On such premises there is no escape from rigid determinism. Descartes, as usual when in extreme difficulties, used God to save free will, but the problems of determinism, causality, and absolute space and time were inseparable from his presentation. The attempt to reduce all material phenomena to a single system of one ultimate type of substance obeying mathematical laws of motion set an ideal for science, but only at the cost of handing over to philosophy the elements that could not be fitted in.

As Dr. C. D. Broad puts it: " Science has been able to make the great strides which it has made by deliberately ignoring one side of reality. . . . In philosophy, as in economics, facts do not cease to be real by being ignored ; and the philosopher becomes the residuary legatee of all those aspects of reality which the physicist (quite rightly for his own purpose) has decided to leave out of account " (*Scientific Thought.*)

Useful References

The Metaphysical Foundations of Science, by E. A. Burtt.
Dialogues Concerning Two Great Systems of the World, *by* Galileo ; 1632.
Novum Organum, by Francis Bacon ; 1620.
Leviathan, by Thomas Hobbes, Intro. by M. Oakeshott ; 1946.
The Philosophical Works of Descartes, trs. by Haldane and Ross, 2 vols ; 1911–12.
A Discourse on Method, by Descartes ; Everyman edition.

CHAPTER FOUR

Architects of the Universe

IN the seventeenth century physics slipped its moorings from philosophy before anyone quite realized the significance of what had happened. Philosophers still went on talking about physical problems; and for centuries they went on talking about psychological and sociological problems. It is only comparatively recently that psychology and sociology have become subjects in their own right, unamenable to armchair methods; and even now there is no agreed set of concepts.

Experimental philosophy did not perfect its method at a single stroke. It became aware of what it was doing very gradually, as it dropped unprofitable methods. The progress of science has been marked by a slow, self-clarification under the watchful and often jealous eye of the philosopher. The latter was finally left as a solitary spectator of the young sciences, which were boisterously self-confident and somewhat contemptuous of their elderly parent.

To the scientist the philosopher has often seemed superfluous, because of his inability to contribute any specific knowledge. But the seventeenth-century Rationalists can scarcely be accused of undue modesty in their aims. Their massive systems stand behind us like audacious Towers of Babel. The metaphysicians themselves appear as architects of the very universe. They claim to give a ground-plan of the whole of reality.

We are not called upon to-day to choose between their rival systems. The value of their mighty efforts is not to be measured simply as success or failure. No one in the seventeenth century—any more than in the twentieth or the fiftieth—could be expected to provide a ground-plan of the whole of reality.

But the struggle with these tremendous problems brought new and extremely useful ideas to light. Trains of thought were started which can be picked up to-day and enable us to re-state the fundamental issues more and more clearly.

The Method of Rationalism

What is far more important for us to grasp than the details of the systems of the great metaphysicians is the procedure that they were trying out. They were Rationalists in the philosophical sense of the word ; that is to say, they believed that knowledge could be obtained merely by the act of reasoning, and that such knowledge was independent of experience. If it seemed to be contradicted by the senses, so much the worse for the senses ; what alone would be fatal to such knowledge would be a logical contradiction.

To-day this is not only a highly unpopular doctrine, but it requires a considerable effort to understand all that it implies. We, for example, regard the scientific account of the universe as being at the mercy of experience. If fresh observations do not fit in with a scientific theory, we do not ignore the observations ; we abandon the theory. For most of us scientific knowledge is an explanation, or a correlation, of experience, and we do not think that we can obtain sufficient experience by sitting in an armchair and reflecting. The early Rationalist, however, could justify his sedentary habits only by claiming that there was information ready waiting, so to speak, inside his head. By looking inside he believed that he could discover the bricks and the general plan of the universe. He did not create these bricks and trim them to observed facts ; they were already in his mind, and the facts were what he trimmed.

The so-called facts were therefore regarded as second-hand representations of reality rather than slices of reality directly perceived. Colours, smells, noises were located in the human body, not in external nature. Descartes agreed with Galileo on this point ; and Leibniz went much farther, and asserted that all the appearances of matter—even space and time—were delusive. Spinoza declared that we were deceived by the

D

" imagination," which showed us things in isolation, and that the reason corrected this error by showing us things in their inter-connectedness.

Paradoxical as it sounds, Rationalism of this sort is possible only if we assume the correctness of basic intuitions. And in the seventeenth century the most certain of these intuitions seemed to be the existence of God.

Words change their meanings. To-day we do not associate Rationalism with a belief that the existence of God is self-evident. But it was otherwise with Descartes, Spinoza, and Leibniz. They undoubtedly used the omnipotence of God to cover up the weaknesses in their systems ; but they were by no means ashamed of doing so. God seemed much more certain to them than the reality of the external world.

They felt that to reason at all you must have some fixed starting-point. You cannot obtain certitude if you start from an assumption ; and certitude was what they sought—the kind of certainty which mathematics seemed to possess. Their " proofs " of God's existence amount to demonstrations that it cannot be denied without contradiction. Descartes, for example, did not prove the existence of God from the existence of the world ; he turned the famous traditional proof upside down and argued that we were certain that the world existed because God was incapable of deceiving us. Take away God and the external world might well be *maya*.

Leibniz could think of no explanation of the order of nature apart from God. Hence his doctrine of the Pre-established Harmony of Monads. For Spinoza, God was practically another name for the universe, and therefore God's existence was indubitable. We, as aspects of the world, states of the single Substance, become conscious of the reason and the order which we exemplify ; we are aware of the ground of reason, which is in our own natures, for the existence of which no reason can be given.

Spinoza (1632–1677) is perhaps the most uncompromising Rationalist of all the metaphysicians. Unlike Descartes and Leibniz, he was under no compulsion to adapt his ideas to

Christian theology. Brought up as a Jew, he inherited an alien intellectual tradition, and there is some reason to believe that he was influenced by the Arabic school, especially by Maimonides (1135–1204).

We are not now concerned with the intricate details of his system, but with his essential ideas, which opened up a fascinating new pathway that did not begin to be explored for a century and a half after his death.

The Monistic Solution

Spinoza shared the Cartesian longing for an account of the whole structure of reality that was as certain as mathematical knowledge, but he saw one great weakness in Descartes' argument. In his anxiety to show that God was the continuous support of the world of flux, Descartes was driven towards an atomic view of Time. He felt that if the future of the world depended solely on its antecedent state, there would be nothing for God to do, once the world had been created. Every moment Time seemed to annihilate the world; therefore, continuous creative intervention of God alone could guarantee the conformity of the future to the past.

Descartes was wrestling, of course, with the old problem of change; but to Spinoza it was as arbitrary to account for the order of nature by continuous divine intervention as to assert that there were two, and only two, utterly distinct substances. Spinoza argued that without an order of nature there could be no scientific knowledge; unless the universe was rational it could not be explored by reason, and he could not accept a perpetual miracle to preserve the appearance of rationality. By equating the universe with God he gave a new meaning to laws of nature. They were not transcendental—imposed from outside—but immanent, or expressions of internal relationships. Nothing was supernatural; everything was a system of logical ground and consequent. The laws of nature must express the real connections between things that are found within nature. In a sense, laws are the thoughts of God, and the universe is the body of God. The test of whether a law is true is therefore a rational inquiry as to whether it fits into a harmonious pattern. Spinoza was the first serious sponsor of the coherence theory of Truth.

To speak of a " a thing," according to Spinoza, is to make a false abstraction. There are no separate " things." There are no separate " substances." A substance, as Descartes says, " requires nothing but itself in order to exist "; but for Spinoza this is tantamount to a definition of God. For what else but God can require *nothing but itself* in order to exist ? God is that, the non-existence of which cannot be conceived. You cannot think of anything else without immediately realizing that it is dependent on yet another thing ; God is the whole series of so-called things, he is Everything—the One which we misperceive as the Many.

Just as there are no independent things, so there are no independent ideas ; there is, rigorously speaking, only one Idea. For whatever you think of leads on to something else with which it is related. Begin with any idea you please, you will be driven along the dialectical path that leads to the One, the Totality, or—as it seemed to later philosophers who adopted this method of reasoning—to the Absolute. What seems to us independent exists only in an adjectival sense. There is only one Subject, but an infinity of adjectives.

Descartes' thought and extension are not genuine substances, according to Spinoza. They are but attributes of the one Substance. Their particular manifestations are described by him as modes. The relation between body and mind illustrates the relationship between thought and extension throughout the universe. There is no modification of mind without a modification of the body ; and so the realm of matter is not dead, as Descartes believed ; it is animated by God.

Nor do thought and extension exhaust the richness of the single Totality. Those are the only two attributes we are able to know, but there is an infinity of attributes ; nevertheless, because they are all predicates of a single subject, there is only one universe. To take an analogy that could scarcely have occurred to Spinoza, the reality unperceived by the human mind nevertheless exists, like a fourth dimension unperceived by a three-dimensional being.

The consequences of this view for ethics are startling, and they were ruthlessly drawn by Spinoza. When we look at the world as a rational whole, *sub specie aeternitatis* (under the form of eternity), we reach a standpoint beyond good and evil. Effects follow causes according to the unbreakable determinism of the divine Reason. Our happiness depends on how clearly we comprehend this necessity; to fail to understand it is to think confusedly. Emotional or imaginative thinking is confused (inadequate); but rational thinking is clear (adequate). The highest possible happiness is to attain cosmic consciousness, to be filled with elevated joy at the sublime spectacle of the unity of all reality as an expression of immanent law.

This stupendous conception has dazzled men's minds like the enchantments of Plato. It is worth all the effort required to rise to it, just as the appreciation of great poetry or great music is supremely worth while for its own sake.

Spinoza, of course, was execrated in his lifetime. He was excommunicated by the synagogue and generally condemned as an Atheist. He seems to have borne the scurrilous abuse poured upon him with the philosophical calm that he recommended to others. Few philosophers, it must be confessed, have shown such persistent nobility of character. Refusing legacies and pensions, he earned a frugal livelihood as a grinder of lenses, and all that we know of his life shows him to have been sincere, indifferent to personal advancement, and scrupulously honest. He followed the light of reason with a fearlessness that may be contrasted with the following admission by Descartes—no doubt with one eye upon the Catholic Church : " We ought to submit to divine authority rather than to our own judgment, even though the light of reason may seem to suggest with the utmost clearness and evidence something else." (*Principles of Philosophy*, I, 76.)

How much of Spinoza's system can be accepted to-day ? This is a natural enough question to ask, but the point is really whether any of the concepts that he clarified (we cannot say originated) have stood the test of time. The immanence of law and the idea of the unity of the universe are still significant ; though, since we have the choice, most people who use that concept in science would prefer to speak of Nature rather than of God. Determinism, cause and effect, and the " substance-attribute " mode of formulation in general, have come under heavy fire. The whole procedure of Rationalism was soon to be challenged ; but, before considering the attack on his method, let us glance at the very different results achieved by Leibniz, following a similar procedure.

The Pluralistic Solution

Leibniz (1646–1716) was a very much less attractive character than Spinoza, though the charge that he plagiarized some of Spinoza's ideas, like the even more serious accusation that he stole Newton's discovery of the Calculus, is undoubtedly baseless. He, too, was an amateur philosopher ; he was very much a man of affairs, a courtier and historian as well as a mathematician. His philosophy at first glance seems so outrageous and perverse that the modern reader would be tempted to dismiss it if he did not suddenly notice, beneath the fanciful language, certain ideas that are surprisingly recognizable in the writings of some contemporary physicists and philosophers. In his lifetime Leibniz quarrelled with Newton, and until quite recently it was assumed that Leibniz was not merely wrong but guilty of lèse-majesté. In a sense it now seems that Leibniz was right and Newton wrong, for the quarrel was largely about absolute space and absolute time, both of which concepts have been since abandoned by physics.

Spinoza sacrificed the Many to the One ; Leibniz the One to the Many. Spinoza gives the impression of ranging through inter-stellar spaces with a mighty telescope, opening up vistas of universes beyond all reckoning ; Leibniz gives the impression of looking through a microscope and discovering universes in miniature, " infinity in a grain of sand."

Spinoza encourages a false and dangerous feeling that it is easier to imagine his sort of world than Leibniz's. The truth is that neither can be imagined, but Leibniz runs counter to exceedingly obstinate mental prejudices. In trying to think with Leibniz we seem to be forced against the grain of language —as indeed we are.

And yet there are a number of common-sense beliefs which Leibniz defends and which Spinoza rejects. If " things," in the last analysis, are states of a single substance, how is it that such adjectives as ourselves can feel like nouns ? For that is really what it amounts to. What becomes of individuality, personality, freedom ? If everything is God, are we to say that God has illusions ?

Spinoza tried hard to forestall such objections ; my point now is that whether he succeeded or not, his analysis still seems to run counter to our instinctive beliefs, and Leibniz must not be condemned because he runs against quite different instinctive beliefs.

For Leibniz, freedom and individuality were facts. He could account for them only by returning, with a difference, to the atomism which Spinoza repudiated. He believed, as a Rationalist, in innate ideas. That meant that the truth about the universe, the nature of its bricks, and the secret of their organization, must be discoverable by looking into his own mind. The trouble about this procedure, we may well feel, is that different philosophers find different innate ideas ; but each of them can retort that the others do not look hard enough, or fail to interpret properly what they find.

Descartes had seen God, substance, thought, extension, and self. So, in a sense, had Leibniz, but his interpretation was vastly different. Spinoza had no theological axe to grind and was not greatly troubled by freewill. It was otherwise with Descartes. And Leibniz tried to show what would follow if God had created a world of free individuals. There could be no half-way house such as Dualism, in that event ; each individual, if it were free, if it were exempt not merely from constraint but from metaphysical necessity, would be a separate substance.

But it would not be something passive, a mere substratum

which received various qualities, and which could be stripped of those qualities and continue to exist. It would be active. It would have a specific nature and it would express that nature in its activity. Its striving would make it analogous to force rather than to inert matter. As an individual it would have a special kind of unity—not the unity of a compound, but the unity of an organic whole. An atom conceived as a material particle can be divided and sub-divided ; never mind how many times you cut it in half, it is still a material particle. But you cannot divide up an organic unity without annihilating it.

Such a unity, incapable of sub-division, is called a " simple," in contrast to a compound. Later on we shall meet with the different notion of logical simples—irreducible ideas, out of which a picture of the world can be constructed. Leibniz analysed the universe into simple substances, irreducible organic wholes, unities of forces analogous to individual minds ; by his own definition these were separate substances—that is to say, they were strictly independent of each other. Each existed in its own right ; each was solely concerned with expressing its own nature. These non-spatial, irreducible unities he called monads.

The Viewpoint of a Monad

It is a difficult conception. We certainly cannot imagine it, It is a product of reason. As far as that goes, can we imagine a mathematical point ? Clearly we cannot, yet we make use of the idea and soon stop worrying about the difficulty of imagining it. It can be conceived, though not imagined, and belongs to the ideal world which reason constructs.

We must not think of a monad as in any way resembling a material atom. It is outside of space and time. Monads are not next to each other, in a spatial sense, any more than ideas are. How can we form any notion of them ? Since each of us is a monad, however, we merely have to look at ourselves.

I am sitting in a room, and I can look through a window at people crossing the street. I can look up at the sky and see the sun. I can think of Shakespeare and Julius Cæsar and yesterday's lunch. Yet all this is *in* my mind. The sun is in my mind; so are other people, so are Shakespeare and Julius Cæsar. I have a twinge of toothache; but I cannot feel the toothache of the man crossing the street, and he cannot feel mine. In other words, I am locked in my private world. I know only my own experiences. They are orderly and intelligible. They constitute a unity. I cannot receive anyone else's experiences. I am a monad.

The problem of Solipsism, or how we can know of the existence of what we do not experience, did not trouble Leibniz; he disclosed the problem almost accidentally by describing what seems at first sight a contradiction in terms, a whole universe of solipsists. In the last resort theology could be invoked to account for the existence of other people, other solipsists. God could always get him out of his difficulties; and God was not conceived as a hypothesis, to explain the origin of the external universe. God and the experience of self were part of the data. God was not an assumption, but a " stubborn fact " found by reason.

Let us pause for a moment and consider where this unusual way of looking at things takes us. If it be granted that God and substance are inescapable ideas, then by exploring their meaning we can deduce a community of simple, indivisible substances, a society of solipsists. The reader, confronted with this conception for the first time, may reluctantly admit that *part* of the universe can be thought of in this curious fashion, but he will protest that a very big part has been left out. Material objects have been left out. We seem to be offered a society of minds without bodies, without animals or vegetables or minerals; surely Leibniz cannot mean that lumps of rock, tables, and chairs are not really composed of material particles, but are assemblages of minds?

Yet that is what he does mean. Leibniz is no less ruthless than Spinoza in carrying his logic to its surprising conclusion. The paper on which I am writing, the desk on which it rests, the room in which I sit, are assemblages of minds, according to Leibniz. Does this mean that the pen with which I write is

conscious ?   No, Leibniz does not mean anything quite as outrageous as that.   The pen is composed of monads, and monads
are minds, but to be a mind it is not necessary to be conscious.
Does not the modern psychologist talk of unconscious mind ?

Very well, let even this be granted.   How can compounds
of minds yield the experience of solid, coloured, noisy, moving
objects ?   Leibniz is not embarrassed by this question, for both
Descartes and Galileo have extracted secondary qualities from
the world disclosed by reason.   Once such a step has been
taken it is easy enough to go still farther and assert that *all* the
appearances of matter are delusive.

In his own words : " I hold space and also time to be something purely relative.   Space is an order of co-existences, as
time is an order of successions.   Space denotes in terms of
possibility an order of things which, in so far as they exist together, exist at the same time, whatever be their several ways of
existing.   Whenever we see various things together we are
conscious of this order between things themselves."

The Problem of Knowledge

No sooner do we lose patience with Leibniz, because he
seems to say something utterly fantastic, than we are arrested
by a phrase, a turn of thought of astonishing modernity.   We
get a vivid impression of a man with incredibly penetrating insight, struggling with the inevitable limitations and theological
prejudices of his age.   He saw quite clearly that it was arbitrary
to divide the universe into Thought and Extension, Primary and
Secondary qualities.   Either individuality had to be abandoned, and you had to go forward with Spinoza to the one, all-
devouring Reality ; or you had to retain the individuality of
the Many and drop the common-sense notion of matter.
Leibniz makes more explicit the distinction between the two
worlds—Common-sense and Reason, Appearance and Reality.
He paves the way for Kant's distinction between noumena,
or things in themselves, and phenomena, or things as experienced.

Leibniz opens up the problem of Idealism.   He is commonly regarded as a Pluralist (believing in many substances) in the sense that Spinoza was a Monist (believing in one substance). We can almost say that Spinoza regarded the whole universe as a Monad, whereas Leibniz regarded God as the Supreme Monad (*Monas Monadum*), and the creator of a universe of separate monads, quite incapable of acting on each other, each attending to its own affairs, yet mutually adjusted like synchronized clocks, at the instant of creation, so that they could function in compounds (bodies) with the delusive appearance of physical interaction.

Their synchronization was the most dubious part of his scheme. By treating knowledge as a representation in the mind, rather than as direct perception of an external world, he set the stage for a thorough-going Idealism ; but this very insistence that the monads were blind and could not influence each other as atoms were supposed to do led to problems that he could not solve without invoking God. This aspect of the Monadology has no special significance for us to-day. We may ask, however, how he supposed that an individual mind could even formally represent to itself the whole society of monads if, as he says, " the monads have no windows by means of which anything can enter in or pass out ? "

Once again there is a refreshing modernity in Leibniz's solution. The monads do not interact, according to the strictly physical principle of action and reaction ; but that does not mean that they cannot communicate. When someone gives me an idea, it is not as though he gave me a pint of his blood ; ideas do not literally pass in and out of our minds.

Each monad is a system of force, rather than of matter ; it is a system of activities. Its freedom is limited only by the existence of other equally free systems of self-activity. This mutual limitation is *interpreted* by the monad as knowledge of the external world. By reason of its divinely appointed status in the totality of monads each individual monad mirrors the whole, more or less imperfectly.

Thus, according to the clarity or confusedness of its perception, each monad has its place in a hierarchy ; there are the unconscious perceptions of a stone, rising in stages through the vegetable and animal orders to the conscious apperceptions of the rational monad, and the still clearer ideas of angels and archangels, and so on until we reach God. A stone, or a human body, forms a compound in the hierarchy under a dominant monad. Although this part of the theory seems remote enough from modern problems, it is of interest to note that McDougall has found the conception of a dominant monad of some value in psychology.

It is impossible in a brief summary to do more than indicate some of the most interesting features of Leibniz's thought. At every turn he seems to uncover new and fascinating ideas.

Kant picked up the thread that the mind constructs a formal pattern of reality and does not give us a picture of things-in-themselves. The notion of a windowless monad, once the theological structure is cut away, carries us into the perplexities of Subjective Idealism. Another most fruitful suggestion was that a thing is what it does—which leads us towards Whitehead's universe of events, instead of passive quality-bearing substances.

The relational theory of space and time would have made Leibniz more at ease in the presence of Einstein than of Newton (apart from their personal feud); and he would not have been so distressed as Spinoza about the self-sufficient electron. He would certainly have been at home in the company of psychologists who speak of " unconscious minds." He would have appreciated Wittgenstein's argument for logical simples, but he would have been greatly shocked by his repudiation of metaphysics.

That many modern conceptions were latent in Leibniz must not blind us to the deep cleavage between much of seventeenth-century and twentieth-century thought. The theological background has vanished and the scientists have made tremendous inroads into the happy hunting-ground over which the philosopher once roamed.

We do not read Leibniz or Spinoza nowadays in order to discover how the universe works. We can, however, read them for the peculiar intellectual excitement they give, for an enjoyment which is none the less deep because it may not materially add to our knowledge. No mere summary of their ideas can give the intense intellectual satisfaction of following in detail not the working of the universe, but the process of rare minds grappling with the profoundest of problems—Spinoza, trying to show how the world must appear to God, and Leibniz (in Whitehead's apt phrase), trying to show what it feels like to be an atom.

The first adventure of Rationalism was one of the most daring assaults of the human mind. It was an attempt to demonstrate the power of reason by deducing the nature of the universe from some self-validated concepts believed to be implicit in the mind. We were thought to carry an answer-book within us, as it were. But suppose that, after all, the answers were not already buried in the mind ? Suppose we were not endowed with these basic concepts out of which we could construct a ground plan of the universe with confidence that it was not a mere work of the imagination ? If the Rationalist procedure was invalid, how else could we attain the certainty for which Descartes longed ?

The whole of this method was challenged by John Locke. He raised the disturbing question of how our ideas—the bricks with which we construct our system of Reality—are obtained. He was led to deny the existence of innate ideas—which were the foundations of deductive Rationalism. The denial led to the formation of a rival school of thought, Empiricism.

USEFUL REFERENCES

Life and Philosophy of Spinoza, by F. Pollock ; 1880.
A Study of Spinoza's Ethics, by H. H. Joachim ; 1901.
Spinoza's Ethics and De Intellectus Emendatione ; Everyman edition.
Leibniz, by H. Wildon Carr ; 1929.
A Critical Exposition of the Philosophy of Leibniz, by Bertrand Russell ; 1900.
The Monadology and Other Writings, by Leibniz, trs. by R. Latta ; 1898.

CHAPTER FIVE

The Revolt Against Metaphysics

ONE evening in the winter of 1670 half a dozen men sat together in a room in London discussing various problems of morality and religion. They could make no progress. " After we had awhile puzzled ourselves," Locke relates, " without coming any nearer a resolution of those doubts which perplexed us, it came into my thoughts, that we took a wrong course ; and that, before we set ourselves upon inquiries of that nature, it was necessary to examine our own abilities, and see what objects our understandings were or were not fitted to deal with. This I proposed to the company, who all readily assented, that this should be our first inquiry."

At the next meeting, Locke says, he produced " some hasty and undigested thoughts on a subject I had never before considered." But the matter could not rest there ; Locke was committed to an inquiry which resulted in the epoch-making *Essay Concerning Human Understanding* and laid the foundations of a new branch of philosophy—Epistemology, or the Theory of Knowledge.

John Locke (1632–1704) was born in Somersetshire, ten years before Newton and the beginning of the Civil War, and sixteen years after the death of Shakespeare. The first edition of the *Essay* was published in 1690, and the final version (with important additions) in 1700. It matured slowly during a period of tumultuous happenings and tremendous intellectual activity. The world was changing its shape, and Locke himself was caught up in the flux of events. After the disgrace of his patron, Lord Shaftesbury, he took refuge for a while in Holland under an assumed name.

On the whole, however, he had a comfortable life, and held

a number of lucrative public offices. No doubt he found these more profitable than the practice of medicine, but his training as a physician left its mark on his speculations. In later years, freed from financial worries, he could contemplate the intellectual ferment of his day with detachment.

He entered the debate as an amateur, but he brought into it the eye for practical detail of a doctor and administrator, and the robust if sometimes complacent common-sense that characterized an age of expanding prosperity. He was sturdily resolved to bring philosophy down to earth. " In an age that produces such masters as the great Huygenius, and the incomparable Mr. Newton, with some other of that strain, it is ambition enough to be employed as an under-labourer in clearing ground a little, and removing some of the rubbish that lies in the way to knowledge ; which certainly had been very much more advanced in the world, if the endeavours of ingenious and industrious men had not been much cumbered with the learned but frivolous use of uncouth, affected, or unintelligible terms introduced into the sciences, and there made an art of to that degree, that philosophy, which is nothing but the true knowledge of things, was thought unfit or uncapable to be brought into well-bred company and polite conversation."

The Problem of Language

What is the " rubbish " to which he contemptuously refers ? It is partly the remains of Aristotelianism, partly the jargon of the medieval Schoolmen, and partly certain aspects of the then fashionable Cartesianism. He does not appear to have been interested in either Spinoza or Leibniz, and although the latter sent Locke a very detailed criticism of the *Essay*, Locke died before he could reply. We may assume, however, that he would not have had much patience with the abstruse conceptions of the Monadology. He was opposed to the whole procedure of the metaphysicians. It seemed to him a disease of language.

Therein lies the novelty of Locke. He challenged the validity of the prevailing method of philosophy. He saw with extraordinary clearness that many of the traditional problems were only pseudo-problems. They were arguments about words. " The greatest part of the questions and controversies that perplex mankind depend on the doubtful and uncertain use of words." Again : " There is scarce any sect in philosophy has not a distinct set of terms that others understand not. But yet this gibberish, which in the weakness of human understanding, serves so well to palliate men's ignorance and cover their errors, comes by familiar use among those of the same tribe to seem the most important part of language."

The words that instantly arouse his wrath are Substance, Genera, Species, and Essence. He claims that instead of studying real facts the metaphysicians studied names and pretended to extract knowledge from empty sounds. Thus they constructed a world of reason that had no contact with the world of ordinary experience. Words, according to Locke, are conventional signs upon which we agree for the purpose of intercourse. They represent ideas ; but they do not, of course, resemble ideas. By making marks on paper or uttering sounds we excite in others the ideas which the words signify for us.

It would be quite impossible for every specific thing to have a particular name. The uniqueness of each individual thing and of each personal experience cannot be directly communicated. Somehow we have to construct an inter-subjective world for the purpose of discourse. We do so by the device of inventing general terms. All things that exist are only particulars ; but by a process of abstraction we can make general names—man, animal, horse, metal, for example. What distinguishes a particular individual from his neighbour can be ignored ; the concept is formed, as a labour-saving device, so that we can distinguish a man from a horse or a piece of iron.

The problem of the existence of Universals, which led to the controversy between the Realists and Nominalists, is fictitious, according to Locke. Universals do not exist ; they are linguistic abstractions. Particulars alone exist. " This is that which in short I would say, viz., that all the great business of genera and species, and their essences, amounts to no more but this—that men making abstract ideas, and settling them in their minds, with names annexed to them, do thereby enable themselves to consider things, and discourse of them, as it were, in bundles, for the easier and readier improvement and communication of their knowledge; which would advance but slowly, were their words and thoughts confined only to particulars."

The Sources of Knowledge

What exactly are these particulars, that the mind assembles into bundles or classes, of which words are the signs? Locke calls them ideas—a term which must be examined carefully. He does not use it in Plato's sense. "Every man being conscious to himself, that he thinks, and that which his mind is applied about, whilst thinking, being the ideas that are there, it is past doubt that men have in their mind several ideas, such as are those expressed by the words, ' whiteness, hardness, sweetness, thinking, motion, man, elephant, army, drunkenness.' "

These ideas are the objects of the thinking subject. They are the crude materials of knowledge. Our knowledge is limited by the number of ideas we possess. They come from two sources: some are the effects of causes outside the mind, others are due to observation of the workings of the mind on what enters from outside. Thus we do not directly perceive what is outside the mind. Our consciousness does not reflect the external world like a mirror. Simple ideas are not, in the main, copies of external things, but signs of them, just as words do not resemble the ideas to which they refer, but are signs of them.

As Locke puts it: "Let us then suppose the mind to be, as we say, white paper, void of characters, without any ideas; how comes it to be furnished? Whence comes it by that vast store, which the busy and boundless fancy of man has painted on it with an almost endless variety? Whence has it all the materials of reason and knowledge? To this the answer is, in

E

one word, From experience : in that all our knowledge is founded, and from that it ultimately derives itself. Our observation, employed either about external sensible objects, or about internal operations of our minds, perceived and reflected on by ourselves, is that which supplies our understandings with all the materials of thinking. These two are the fountains of knowledge, from whence all the ideas we have, or can naturally have, do spring."

Observation and experience give us our knowledge and set its boundaries. This is the doctrine of Empiricism, as opposed to deductive Rationalism. It expresses the spirit of the new experimental philosophy. " The metaphysicians," wrote Roger Cotes in a preface to the second edition of Newton's *Principia*, " being entirely employed in giving names to things, and not in searching into things themselves, we may say that they have invented a philosophical way of speaking, but not that they have made known to us true Philosophy."

The barren search for occult qualities and essences seemed to be at an end. As Newton wrote : " To tell us that every Species of things is endowed with an occult, specific quality, by which it acts and produces manifest effects, is to tell us nothing."

Primary and Secondary Ideas

Observe and experiment, ran the new order of the day. Look at the facts, not at the words which merely represent them. But here was a dilemma, for how can you look at facts if the objects of knowledge are not things in the external world, but merely the signs of things ? Having got past one set of signs (words), it seemed at first as though the philosopher was halted by a Chinese wall of another set of signs (ideas).

Locke saw this difficulty. He was not a Subjectivist. He takes it for granted that there is an outside world. The objects in this real world affect our senses. They have the power (from which he derives the notion of cause) to give rise to certain ideas ; they are like a metal seal, and we are the wax.

The pattern is the outcome of that sort of die and our sort

of wax. For example, beings differently constituted, with quite other senses than ours, would get very different ideas of the real world. But the knowledge we have is not illusory ; the modification of our field of consciousness is itself a fact of nature. We are contrived as we are for nature's own purposes.

And *some* of the ideas imprinted on the mind do correspond to the characters possessed by external things. To explain this Locke draws a distinction, between idea and quality. " Whatsoever the mind perceives in itself, or is the immediate object of perception, thought or understanding, that I call ' idea ' ; and the power to produce any idea in our mind, I call ' quality ' of the subject wherein the power is."

Locke therefore accepts the distinction made by Galileo and Descartes between objective and subjective qualities. " Original or Primary Qualities " are said to be what we cannot think away, what is utterly inseparable from the object, despite all the changes it undergoes. They amount to a description of matter. They produce in us such simple ideas as solidity, extension, figure, motion, and number. Secondary qualities " are nothing in the objects themselves, but powers to produce various sensations in us by their primary qualities."

The ideas of primary qualities resemble the external objects. If our senses were acute enough the secondary qualities of the bodies we observe would disappear, and we would be able to contemplate the primary qualities. But Locke, with his dry common-sense, adds that even if " by the help of such microscopical eyes a man could penetrate farther than ordinary into the secret composition and radical texture of bodies, he would not make any great advantage by the change, if such an acute sight would not serve to conduct him to the market and exchange."

Nothing was known of biology and evolution in the seventeenth century. Locke, however, could have given guarded assent to the following quotation from a contemporary work of philosophy, though he would have substituted God for Nature : " Nature, in determining the character of the animal organism, of its sense-organs and nervous system generally, has had in view primarily only the self-preservation of the species.   Yet in following this path, she has also made possible the acquiring of knowledge.   In preparing such knowledge as is of aid in survival—allowing no more knowledge than is indispensable for this purpose—she has in man brought into existence, or at least liberated, a type of sense-experience which, when reinforced by instruments of precision, when sifted and tested by all manner of indirect experimental devices, yields data sufficient for the attaining of scientific insight." (*Prolegomena to an Idealist Theory of Knowledge*, N. Kemp Smith.)

The Boundaries of Knowledge

Locke believed that our knowledge of nature is restricted to ideas which come from outside through the senses, and to which we are powerless to add.   Leibniz, it will be recalled, took exactly the opposite view—that the monads are windowless, and all knowledge is an elucidation of what is already implicit in the mind.   For Locke, however, " unconscious perception " is a contradiction in terms.   The mind is active in abstracting and combining to frame complex ideas, but no ideas are latent in it.

The raw material of knowledge consists, therefore, in those simple ideas which are excited by the action of the external world on the senses, and in those ideas which arise from the operation of the mind itself on these sensations.   The latter is reflective knowledge, and Locke likens it to " internal sense " ; it is our experience of thinking and willing.   Thus we have : (A) the powers and qualities that exist in the external world ; (B) the powers and operations of the mind ; (C) simple ideas of sensation and reflection ; (D) composite ideas and abstractions derived from simple ideas by the activity of the mind.

It is impossible, as he frankly acknowledges, to construct a ground-plan of the entire universe out of such elements, or to produce any scheme that has the certainty of mathematics. Locke disavows any such ambitions.   Having searched for evidence of innate ideas and found none, he is unable to escape with Descartes from the confusion and unreliability of the senses into a logical realm where everything is exact and impeccably demonstrable. He has no window of intuition through which he can glimpse a deeper reality than that disclosed by experience. He has denied the existence of any such short cut to truth. As he insists : " I must appeal to experience and observation whether I am in the right ; the best way to come to truth being to examine things as really they are, and not to conclude they are as we fancy of ourselves, or have been taught by others to imagine."

Again, in a passage the modesty of which contrasts (perhaps ironically) with the grandiose aims of the metaphysicians : " I pretend not to teach, but to inquire, and therefore cannot but confess here again, that external and internal sensation are the only passages that I can find of knowledge to the understanding. These alone, as far as I can discover, are the windows by which light is let into this dark room. For methinks the understanding is not much unlike a closet wholly shut from light, with only some little openings left to let in external visible resemblances or ideas of things without ; would the pictures coming into such a dark room but stay there, and lie so orderly as to be found upon occasion, it would very much resemble the understanding of a man in reference to all objects of sight and the ideas of them."

Where Locke Fails

Locke can be read with enjoyment, and his influence is still strongly felt. The arguments with which he applies his first principles are so subtle and exhaustive that one rises from the spell of his lucidity and the vast sweep of his mind with a feeling that there is little more to be said. Philosophy has been made to speak the language of everyday life ; and the great systems of the metaphysicians seem like elaborate earthworks of wasted ingenuity.

But when we look more closely it becomes evident, unhappily, that Locke has merely started yet another tunnel, from another side of the same mountain into which all philosophers have been burrowing. It is a fresh approach, but it only gives

rise to new questions.   There are many flaws in Locke's system.
Let us glance at a few of them.

(1) Is it really the case that all our general notions are
derived from simple ideas ?   It would obviously be desirable
to reduce them to units if possible.   It may be that in making
this attempt Locke was on sound lines, for without mystical
aids it is difficult otherwise to show that the world disclosed by
reason and the world of sense-experience have a common reference.   But parts of Locke's analysis are undoubtedly defective.
His account of space and causation is inadequate ; and although
such ideas as yellow, heat, cold, soft, and hard, can be accepted
as " simple and unmixed," surely we cannot take extension,
solidity, mobility, existence, duration, and motivity as being
" original ideas " on which our knowledge depends.   These,
however, are points of detail, and for the moment we must leave
it an open question whether a satisfactory reduction can be
made.   More serious is Locke's departure from the empirical
method by admitting that some knowledge is intuitive.

(2) Locke holds that we know self by intuition, God by
demonstration, and all else by sensation.   His proof of God's
existence is cosmological ; it is an attempt to demonstrate the
necessity by an appeal to facts, and so he maintains his distance
from the Rationalists who claimed that the existence of God is
a self-evident proposition—in the sense that if we can think of
a perfect being he must exist, for existence is a part of perfection.
" For, the having the idea of anything in our mind no more
proves the existence of that thing than the picture of a man
evidences his being in the world, or the visions of a dream make
thereby a true history."

It did not occur to Locke to try to reduce self to a succession
of sensations.   Hume and Condillac endeavoured to do so, and,
whether they succeeded or no, they were certainly following
the strict empirical method.   Locke departs from its rigour
when he declares : " The knowledge of our own being we have
by intuition."

Admittedly he does not set out to give a theory of the nature
of the mind.   His " ideas of reflection " are ideas of the

operations of the mind, not of the mind itself. But it is important to note his insistence that, although these operations are not produced by sensation, they could not occur without it. If the external world provided no data, the mind would have nothing to be conscious of—a doctrine that would undermine Locke's religious beliefs.

(3) Just as the mind is the ground of ideas, so material substance is the ground of the " powers " and " qualities " of which Locke continually, but rather vaguely, speaks. He appeals to common-sense. " Whilst I write this, I have, by the paper affecting my eyes, that idea produced in my mind which whatever object causes, I call white ; by which I know that that quality or accident (i.e., whose appearance before my eyes always causes that idea) doth really exist and hath a being without me."

One cannot, he protests, think of mere qualities existing together in a bundle. They must have some kind of support. To the question of the Ionians, " What is the world made of ? " it is impossible to reply that it is made of qualities. And so " we accustom ourselves to suppose some substratum wherein qualities do subsist and from which they result ; which therefore we call ' Substance '." The only idea anyone has of substance is " a supposition of he knows not what support of such qualities which are capable of producing simple ideas in us." It is nothing but " the supposed and unknown support of these qualities we find existing."

Locke cannot make a complete break with tradition, and it seems to irritate him. He fights shy of any exact definition of substance because it would almost certainly land him back in metaphysics. And so the reality of the external world is left precariously dependent on an obscure " I know-not-what " and an almost Johnsonian appeal to common-sense.

(4) Finally, Locke is vulnerable in his account of primary and secondary qualities. It was proving a great practical convenience to the scientist to abstract matter and motion from the welter of experience, and substitute them for the traditional categories inherited from Aristotle. But to assert, as Locke

did, that an external reality literally possesses these primary characteristics, that certain of the simple ideas which are the objects of the mind are true copies of the unknown something outside the mind, is not consistent with a rigorous empiricism.

The Outcome of Empiricism

The greatness of Locke's contribution was to challenge the prevailing fashion and to set philosophy on a fresh track. Bacon and Hobbes were like lone explorers, sighting new territory, but Locke arrived, and set about the task of surveying it in a methodical and fairly scientific fashion. The new territory, in a word, was experience. The work of his immediate successors was to investigate what happened when the *whole* of knowledge was restricted to an interpretation of experience. Any attempt to get outside the circle of experienced facts came to be condemned as metaphysics.

The results were somewhat surprising. Locke went to a great deal of trouble to soothe the anxieties of his theological critics, notably the Bishop of Worcester. They feared that " the new way of Ideas " would undermine religious orthodoxy. Locke's own religious beliefs were clear and untroubled ; but there can be little doubt that the Bishop's fears were justified.

Paradoxically enough, those who saw in empiricism a firm support for science were also soon to be disillusioned. It freed science from the shackles of medievalism, but only at a great cost. For it robbed it of all hope of obtaining certitude. The only certain knowledge was contained in our immediate presentations ; all else was interpretation, and merely probable, with the exception of mathematics, which was regarded by Locke (though not by Hume) as ideal.

Neither Locke nor his followers, of course, could foresee the extent to which science would one day transform the world. It had altered man's picture of the universe, but it had not yet made much difference to everyday life. The " microscopical eye," to which Locke refers, had not yet helped men " to go to the market or the exchange " in a railway train, a motor car, or aeroplane, or made any great difference to what they found on arrival.

The rationalist method had made it possible to speak about the universe as a whole ; that was its chief recommendation. When it was abandoned, it was possible to speak only of experiences—they constituted the entire universe. The immediate development of empiricism was therefore a purely subjective philosophy for which an external world was redundant.

What are the limits of the understanding ? asked Locke, at the outset of his inquiry. His final answer gave cold comfort to the scientist. " I deny not but a man accustomed to rational and regular experiments shall be able to see farther into the nature of bodies, and guess righter at their yet unknown properties, than one that is a stranger to them ; but yet, as I have said, this is but judgment and opinion, not knowledge and certainty. This way of getting and improving our knowledge in substances only by experience and history, which is all that the weakness of our faculties in this state of mediocrity which we are in in this world can attain to, makes me suspect that natural philosophy is not capable of being made a science."

The sceptical outcome was inevitable, for " as God has set some things in broad daylight . . . so, in the greatest part of our concernment, he has afforded us only the twilight, as I may so say, of probability." And it was not long before the broad daylight disappeared.

Berkeley seized on the weakness of Locke's doctrine of substance. This mysterious something, this " I-know-not-what," could have no place in a thorough-going empiricism. We have no experience of this substratum supposedly outside ourselves. Why not rest satisfied with the ideas and eliminate the otiose, metaphysical concept of substance ?

Hume was even more drastic. He applied the same sort of criticism to both mind and cause. Locke had stated that the mind's knowledge of itself is intuitive—but what has intuition to do with empiricism ? We are never conscious of the *self*, said Hume ; we are conscious only of its presumed states. We know only the elements, as it were, the atoms of sensation which flicker and vanish. Is not the idea of a self or ego as illegitimate as substance ?

He went still farther. Locke had tacitly assumed the existence of causation. But how do we really *know* that the sun will rise to-morrow ? Surely all that an empiricist can say is that it has done so in the past, and so we have formed a habit of expectation ? What necessary connection is there between one bit of experience and another, so that we can speak of one always *causing* the other ?

This was the catastrophic result of the rejection of metaphysics. The external world was annihilated ; and with it both the self and any possibility of knowledge beyond the presentation of the fleeting instant.

The very structure of reality seemed to collapse, once the metaphysical props had been taken away. It was Kant who tried to rescue the English philosophers from the wreck they had made—and he turned for assistance to Leibniz, who had been forgotten in the commotion.

Useful References

A History of English Philosophy, by W. R. Sorley ; 1937.
An Essay Concerning Human Understanding, by John Locke ; 1690.
New Essays Concerning Human Understanding, by G. W. Leibniz (first published in 1765), is a criticism of Locke's *Essay*. Condillac's *Traité des Sensations* (1754), and *Traité des Systemes* (1749), show a radical development from Locke.

CHAPTER SIX

The Great Dilemma

IT is possible to imagine a man trying to escape from the calamities of a world in dissolution by shutting his eyes and pretending that what is happening is not real. But no such conditions existed at the beginning of the eighteenth century. The English Revolution lay well behind; the ugliness of industrialism was hidden in the future.

The new experimental philosophy had been astonishingly successful. Its exponents could look back contemptuously on the metaphysical quagmires in which bygone philosophers had floundered. They scoffed at the medieval Schoolmen and derided Aristotle—without realizing, however, that they had not freed themselves from all his mistakes. Nevertheless, they had good reason to feel that at last they were on the right track. The veil of mystery was being stripped from the face of nature.

There was little mystery in the world of Addison and Steele, Pope and Defoe; and there was none in the official religion of the period. The emphasis was laid on the reasonableness of Christianity. Locke's essay on this subject appeared in 1695, and in the following year Toland published *Christianity not Mysterious*. Science seemed to supplement, and even confirm, a sober, de-symbolized, Protestant theology. "The eternal silence of these infinite spaces makes me afraid," Pascal had cried; but such foolish fears did not disturb the "polite society," to which Locke addressed himself. Science had disclosed "a mighty maze, but not without a plan," and this reflection was found so comforting that a bust of Newton was placed in Trinity College, Cambridge. He had almost become a saint of the new, intellectually respectable Protestantism.

" Nature and Nature's law lay hid in night ;
God said, Let Newton be ! and all was light."

At first sight, therefore, it seems an odd moment in which to
cast doubts on the reality of the external world. Yet two
philosophers announced, almost simultaneously, their conviction that matter did not exist. Leibniz's *Théodicée* appeared
in 1710, the same year that saw the publication of Berkeley's
Principles of Human Knowledge. The *Monadologie* came out
in 1714, a year after Berkeley's *Three Dialogues between Hylas
and Philonous*. Leibniz, as we have seen, arrived at his conclusion on metaphysical grounds ; Berkeley was driven to his
by trying to iron out the inconsistencies of " the new way of
ideas " ; and so two opposite methods of inquiry, the one
metaphysical, the other empirical, led to a similar verdict—that
the material world is a delusive appearance.

Abstraction and Reality

" I refute it thus ! " exclaimed Dr. Johnson, kicking a large
stone. The plain man may be pardoned for feeling some
impatience with subtle arguments that seem to show that stones
and tables, and the very stars whose movements Newton had
reduced to law, do not really exist. What can this be but
sophistry and a playing with words ? Berkeley had devoted
much of his energy to a project for building a college in Bermuda. Admittedly the college never existed, outside Berkeley's mind, but did he ever doubt the existence of Bermuda ?
Did he doubt the existence of tar-water, which he seemed to
regard as a sovereign cure for most bodily ailments ?

Clearly he did not. Yet if Dr. Johnson, and other plain
men, had taken the trouble to read Berkeley they would have
seen that Immaterialism did not require any such denial of
the evidence of the senses. Berkeley wrote : " I do not argue
against the existence of any one thing that we can apprehend,
either by sense or reflection. That the things I see with my
eyes and touch with my hands do exist, really exist, I make not
the least question. The only thing whose existence we deny

is that which philosophers call matter or corporeal substance. And in doing of this, there is no damage done to the rest of mankind, who, I dare say, will never miss it."

Nothing could be clearer. Stones and tables and stars "exist," because we experience them. Matter, however, is just an abstract noun. You may postulate "matter" but you cannot *experience* it. In the bad old days philosophers had supposed that abstract ideas really did exist, just as savages still believe that names have some mysterious existence and power of their own. To Berkeley this was sheer superstition.

It is unfortunate that the whole discussion was not kept within the sphere of logic and language. Both Locke and Berkeley had seen the enormous importance of investigating the function of words. They rightly regarded words as signs—but signs of what? If we know only particulars, how can we arrive at universals? And if we cannot speak about universals we are reduced to baby-talk.

For example, look at something moving; say, a stone in flight. It describes a parabola. But another moving object may describe a circle or an ellipse or go straight up and down. A single word is required to signify all these happenings. The word employed is " motion." Without such a word Newton could not have stated his famous laws.

Words like " motion," " inertia," " man," " universe," " triangle," are concepts. They are an essential part of our intellectual equipment. Unlike percepts, they are not perceived by the senses, but clearly they may apply to things perceived. Are they constructed out of percepts or are they a part of what is given in our experience?

Locke denied that any concepts are given. He rejected the metaphysical doctrine of innate ideas. He restricted the objects of knowledge to simple ideas, obtained through the senses or by reflection on the mind's own operations. So he had to derive general ideas somehow from simple ideas.

As he puts it, " Since all things that exist are only particulars, how come we by general terms? " He answers that " words become general by being made the signs of general ideas."

And general ideas can be reached by the process of logical abstraction. So reached, they are by no means fictions.

What Words Stand For

General terms, writes Locke, are used " only to save the labour of enumerating the several simple ideas which the next general word or genus stands for." He is unhappy about " substance," but it seems indispensable. It seems to him evident that we must form ideas of material substances, and that they are " such combinations of simple ideas as are taken to represent distinct, particular things subsisting by themselves, in which the supposed or confused idea of substance, such as it is, is always the first and chief. Thus, if to substance be joined the simple idea of a certain dull, whitish colour, with certain degrees of weight, hardness, ductility, and fusibility, we have the idea of lead ; and a combination of the ideas of a certain sort of figure, with the powers of motion, thought and reasoning, joined to substance, make the ordinary idea of a man. Now of substances also there are two sorts of ideas, one of single substances, as they exist separately, as of a man or a sheep ; the other of several of those put together, as an army of men or flock of sheep ; which collective ideas of several substances thus put together, are as much each of them one single idea as that of a man or a unit."

What Berkeley denies is that by blending our ideas we attain a clear, abstract idea, of which the word " substance " is a symbol that can be joined to symbols of simple sense perceptions. We have " the dull, whitish colour, with certain degrees of weight, hardness, ductility, and fusibility "—but that is all. Neither Locke nor Berkeley properly distinguished between the psychological problem of how we in fact form abstractions, and the purely epistemological problem of their status. But the discussion was exceedingly important.

If we say that sense qualities *belong* to or are caused by a material substance, which somehow exists apart from them, we go beyond the evidence, according to Berkeley. The word " lead " stands for just those characteristics, those ideas that

are in the mind.   There is no need to join the characteristics
to the term " substance " in order to get " lead."   Substance
is not a sign that stands for any idea existing in the mind.
Locke himself is very apologetic about it ; he admits that substance is " confused," and well he might.   It is confused,
retorts Berkeley, because it is contradictory, and we cannot in
fact form such an idea, although we may make use of such a
word.

But if there is no need to join predicates to a metaphysical
subject, or to assume that sense qualities are qualities of matter,
there is nothing apart from the images in the consciousness.
In short, there is no material universe, external to the mind ;
and Locke shrank from such an apparently outrageous conclusion.

The possibility of regarding sense-impressions as occurrences,
and of treating all concepts but a very few indefinable and
primitive notions as logical functions of sense-data had yet to
be explored.   It was too early to talk about events and processes
instead of things.   Nevertheless, one result of these discussions
was to show the difficulty of regarding the subject-predicate
form as the only type of proposition.   The paradoxes that
emerged were mainly due to the lingering prejudice that nouns
were somehow more real than verbs.

Inasmuch as Berkeley demonstrated the superfluity of the
concept of substance, he was in the line of advance—though
he would have been perturbed if he could have seen where it
would all end.   Obviously a word like " lead " is very different
from a word like " matter," which seems so much more than a
shorthand device for dealing with collections.   Berkeley regarded matter as a vicious abstraction.   We cannot imagine
man existing, over and above particular men, and so we cannot
regard matter as existing over and above sense-data.   If Locke
merely wanted a cause of sensations, outside ourselves, Berkeley
was ready for him.   God was the author of our ideas, and it
was unnecessary to postulate a world of matter which, in turn,
owed its origin to God.

The justification of Immaterialism is that matter is not an

object of knowledge, but a vicious abstraction. For the ordinary man nothing is altered. He can sleep soundly at night, confident that the sun will rise the next morning. He can leave his house and be assured that it will still be there when he returns. The warmth of the sun and the furniture of his home are not abstractions, but real experiences. If the plain man looks for matter he will not find it; but he will certainly find his bedroom slippers if he wants them.

The Ionian Materialists asked what the world was made of; but to Berkeley this is the wrong question. The "world" is not an immediate object of knowledge, but a construction. What are the objects of knowledge, then? If words are signs, what are their referents? Berkeley's answer is that the ultimate referents of words are ideas. He limited ideas to three classes: (1) ideas actually imprinted on the senses; (2) ideas derived from emotions or mental operations; (3) ideas formed by memory or imagination.

There is no place in this classification for abstract ideas and no place for such a concept as Self. The latter inconsistency is explained as follows: " But besides all that endless variety of ideas, there is likewise something which knows or perceives them, and exercises divers operations, as willing, imagining, remembering about them. This perceiving, active being is what I call mind, spirit, or myself. By which words I do not denote any one of my ideas, but a thing entirely distinct from them, whereby they are perceived, for the existence of an idea consists in being perceived."

The Meaning of Existing

This is the core of Berkeley's teaching, that to say that something exists is to say it is perceived; in his well-known phrase, *esse* is *percipi*. There must be minds to perceive, of course, otherwise the word would be meaningless; apart from minds, all that exists is what is perceived. He goes on, challengingly: " It is indeed an opinion strangely prevailing amongst men, that houses, mountains, rivers and in a word all sensible objects have an existence natural or real, distinct from their being perceived by the understanding." What is believed to be distinct from perception is a mere abstraction.

Such an abstraction is matter, or substance. It is Locke's mysterious " I-know-not-what," a ghostly substratum of which nothing can be affirmed except that it supports qualities. " Matter neither acts, nor perceives, nor is perceived : for this is all that is meant by saying it is an inert, senseless, unknown substance." It is really bare being and practically amounts (as Hegel was to say) to *nothing*. But even if matter existed, we could not become aware of the fact, for how can dead matter excite ideas in mind ? (An ingenious inversion of the usual argument against psycho-physical interaction.) No useful purpose is served by such a concept, and we are merely " amusing ourselves with words."

As Berkeley writes : " Some truths there are so near and obvious to the mind that a man need only open his eyes to see them. Such I take this important one to be, viz., that all the choir of heaven and furniture of the earth, in a word all those bodies which compose the mighty frame of the world, have not any subsistence without a mind, that their *esse* (being) is to be perceived or known ; that consequently so long as they are not actually perceived by me, or do not exist in my mind or that of any other created spirit, they must either have no existence at all, or else subsist in the mind of some eternal spirit : it being perfectly unintelligible and involving all the absurdity of abstraction, to attribute to any single part of them an existence independent of a spirit."

The Appeal to God

From this position Berkeley never budged. We know ideas, but we cannot escape outside that circle. Ideas are what common-sense calls " things." A thing may be compounded of various sensations—touch, smell, taste, hearing, and sight. Suppose, for example, a blind man knew a cube and a sphere only by touch, and suppose his sight were restored. Would he be able to distinguish between the two by sight alone ? Locke held that extension was a simple idea common to both

F

sight and touch; Berkeley, of course, denied this. Nevertheless, Locke inconsistently held that despite this common factor
it would be impossible to recognize a cube and a sphere by sight,
for the first time; Berkeley agreed, but he showed that on
Locke's view of extension it ought to be possible.

Berkeley went too far in his objection to abstraction. Also,
it is quite evident that the knowledge he claimed to have of
spirits and God, to say nothing of scientific laws, cannot be
derived from his threefold division of knowledge into sense,
mental operations, and imagination. Although in the *Principles*
he admits that Spirit, or Self, is not an idea, he does not say
what it is; but in *Hylas* he says that we have an intuitive
knowledge of self and an inferential knowledge of God, spirits,
and laws of nature. This sort of knowledge is not through
ideas, and he calls it *notion*, but he does not develop this line
of thought. It might well have endangered his empiricism.
Similarly, he shied from the possibility that, if existing is being
perceived, then the perceiving mind may not exist when it is
not perceiving.

He was, after all, an Anglican bishop. He could not remain
an orthodox Protestant and hold that all knowledge is restricted
to phenomena. To break out of the solipsistic circle he had to
invoke God. In this way we get a common world and can
distinguish between reality and illusion. "The ideas imprinted on the senses by the Author of nature are called *real
things*," in contrast to those excited in the imagination, which
are "images of things." The laws of nature are the orderly
sequences of God's volitions.

After such an exciting start this seems rather a common-
place conclusion. Berkeley could not transcend the limitations
of his age. What is significant for us to-day is the direction
that Berkeley gave to philosophical inquiry by insisting, more
rigorously than Locke, that the raw material of knowledge is
sensible experience.

But if knowledge is restricted to sense-data, if material substance is dismissed because it lies outside experience, what
justification can be offered for the other abstractions that

science is compelled to use ? Grant that if Immaterialism is correct the plain man will not notice the difference. His house, his furniture, and the kettle on the hob seem just as real, whether they belong to the material world or are just ideas inside his head. But is it only the arbitrary decree of God that makes the water in the kettle boil, instead of turn to ice, when it is heated ? How does the empiricist account for the fact that the assertions of the scientist go far beyond actual experience ?

We have the curious spectacle of the empiricists philosophizing in their studies, extolling experience but avoiding it, while the scientists were experimenting and seeking experience at first hand, although they interpreted it metaphysically. The practical scientist was not troubled about whether matter existed, whether force was a justifiable concept, or whether there was a universal law of causation. He got results even with such dubious concepts as phlogiston. He would have gained nothing by following the empiricists at this stage. In practice the appeal to religion—the reign of law—was more stimulating to science than the appeal to experience, which came to a cul-de-sac with the scepticism of Hume.

" *Strange Monster* "

David Hume (1711–1776) is one of the most remarkable figures in the history of philosophy. No man has ever asked more searching questions ; he did not even pretend to know the answers to the most difficult of them, and, ever since, philosophers have been trying to solve the problems that he bequeathed. According to J. M. Keynes, " Hume's statement of the case against induction has never been improved upon." Prof. L. S. Stebbing held that the problem of causality, as formulated by Hume, has still to be solved. Dr. Carnap acclaims Hume as the father of Logical Positivism.

Some of the philosophers we have considered have very little significance for contemporary thinkers. That is emphatically not the case with Hume, for his stock has never stood higher.

Like Berkeley, he began to think out his philosophy when very young, and, like Locke also, he was an amateur. At the age of eighteen, he says, " there seemed to be opened up to me a new scene of thought, which transported me beyond measure." He had finished *A Treatise of Human Nature* before he was twenty-six, and he was bitterly disappointed with its reception. After he had published *An Inquiry Concerning Human Understanding*, in 1758, he looked back on the *Treatise* as " the juvenile work which the author never acknowledged." He had amended some of his views, and perhaps the frankness of his personal confession brought a blush. " I am first affrighted and confounded with that forlorn solitude in which I am placed in my philosophy, and fancy myself some strange, uncouth monster, who, not being able to mingle and unite in society, has been expelled all human commerce, and left utterly abandoned and disconsolate." He is appalled at his own conclusions. What he thinks in the privacy of his study seems to have no application outside.

By Berkeley the two worlds of common-sense and reason were contrasted as the high road where the illiterate bulk of mankind walk, and the narrow path trodden by the philosopher in the light of a superior principle. For Hume the contrast at times seemed agonizing, and he says that he felt like throwing his books and papers into the fire. " I dine, I play a game of backgammon, I converse and am merry with my friends ; and when, after three or four hours' amusement, I would return to these speculations, they appear so cold, and strained, and ridiculous, that I cannot find it in my heart to enter into them any further." Elsewhere he remarks that he " took a particular pleasure in the company of modest women."

The Objects of Knowledge

Hume was no dry-as-dust philosopher. His freshness and originality, the ruthlessness of his logic, and his utter disregard of religious tradition, brought empiricism temporarily to a standstill. The conclusions he reached seemed intolerable, even to himself, but nobody knew how to refute them.

He accepted Locke's starting-point, that we have no source of knowledge other than simple ideas, sense-data like colours and sounds. He accepted Berkeley's criticism of abstract ideas, but he rejected the exception that Berkeley made in favour of notions. All concepts must be obtained from sense-data.

But he improved upon Locke's terminology. Instead of calling sense-data ideas, he called them impressions. He reserved the word " idea " for what we ordinarily mean by it—a copy either in memory or imagination. Impressions are distinguished from ideas by their greater liveliness—which recalls Berkeley's distinction between images of things and real things, the latter being more vivid and constant.

Impressions arise from unknown causes—though, as we shall see, the word " cause " need not be taken too literally. The point is that all we are acquainted with are impressions. The mind combines its primary ideas (i.e., copies of impressions) in three ways : (1) According to resemblance and contrast, which provides the basis of mathematics ; (2) according to contiguity in space and time, which gives the basis of descriptive and experimental science ; (3) according to causal connection, which gives the basis of what passes beyond mere observation.

Hume believed he had discovered an important law of mental association. It seemed to him that the natural attraction of certain ideas for certain others provided an explanation of the workings of the mind, just as gravitational attraction explained the behaviour of material particles. Instead of being dazzled by a multitude of particular ideas, we are naturally provided with compounds ; for particular ideas swarm together and form a complex idea, and so the trees no longer prevent us from seeing the wood.

We need spend no time on Hume's Law of Association. That is a matter for psychologists, and psychology is no longer an armchair science. But the importance of the logical relation between general and particular ideas cannot be too strongly stressed. If Locke was right, metaphysics is still possible, and such metaphysical concepts as matter and substance may be permitted. But if Berkeley and Hume were right, there is no hope for metaphysics.

What is a Concept?

Consider, yet again, the concept substance. Both Leibniz and Spinoza made it the starting-point of vast metaphysical systems. They analysed the meaning of substance; they showed what concepts were implied by the definition, and they constructed possible universes. But—and this is the point of Hume's criticism—unless the complex concept substance can be shown to contain components that are experiences (impressions), the universes so constructed are like dream castles. To be actual they must be built up of something actual—sense-impressions. A universe made out of ideas, as it were, may be self-consistent, may be possible; but so far from giving us certain knowledge, as the metaphysicians claim, it does not even give us probable knowledge. Probability requires a basis of fact.

This is where the two great schools that we have examined, the Rationalists and the Empiricists, come to a head-on collision. The Rationalists held that the truth of a proposition was established by showing that it necessarily followed from another proposition; the meaning of a concept was contained in another concept. Consequently if you started correctly, if you could discover a sufficiently rich concept, and a sufficiently comprehensive proposition, you had a nest of Chinese boxes from which you could draw out all the other concepts and propositions that were entailed. The only test you needed to apply was of coherence. To be landed in a contradiction was a sign of falsehood. Such, the metaphysicians argued, was the method of mathematics.

The Empiricists admitted that this seemed to be the deductive method of mathematics, but they mostly held that mathematics was a closed system; its propositions were true because its concepts were analytic—nothing was extracted from them that was not already included in them. The conclusion was always buried in the premise.

But it was otherwise with questions of fact. A factual proposition can be upset by the discovery of a new fact. " All crows are black," becomes false if we can produce a white crow. We cannot say that a white crow is unthinkable or a contradiction. The way to test this sort of statement is to see whether it corresponds to the facts. And how can we ever be sure in advance that some new fact, like a white crow, will not turn up to falsify our statement? We may say that it is unlikely; we cannot say that it is impossible.

To sum up, there are "relations between ideas" and "matters of fact." The former give rise to analytic judgments, which lead to a contradiction when denied. They merely tell us what is entailed by an idea; but unless we hold—as some metaphysicians did—that whatever can be thought of exists, analytic judgments can give us no information about the real world.

Propositions which assert facts are synthetic. When they describe an immediate experience, "This is black," they are as certain as analytic judgments. But when they venture beyond immediate experiences, when they generalize, as in "All crows are black," it is possible to deny the proposition without logical contradiction. The truth or falsehood depends on correspondence with facts.

The Complete Sceptic

Such is Hume's basic position, and unless we grasp how he reached it, how profoundly it differs from traditional philosophy, we may be tempted to dismiss his more startling conclusions as attempts to shock us by splitting hairs. The scepticism for which he is famous—and in his lifetime infamous—is merely the logical result of the view that the objects of knowledge are sensible impressions, that we are acquainted with nothing else. If, indeed, all we know are these momentary impressions, how can we be *certain* of what happened yesterday or what will happen to-morrow? We cannot even be certain of the continuous existence of so-called material objects.

Descartes had urged that at least he need not doubt the existence of himself. He took the self as a starting-point because it seemed absolutely certain; but Hume would have none of it. " For my part, when I enter most intimately into what I call *myself*, I always stumble on some particular perception or other, of heat or cold, light or shade, love or hatred, pain or pleasure. I never can catch *myself* at any time without a perception, and never can observe anything but the perception. When my perceptions are removed for any time, as by sound sleep, so long am I insensible of *myself*, and may truly be said not to exist. And were all my perceptions removed by death, and could I neither think, nor feel, nor see, nor love, nor hate, after the dissolution of my body, I should be entirely annihilated, nor do I conceive what is further requisite to make me a perfect nonentity. . . . Setting aside some metaphysicians, I may venture to affirm of the rest of mankind, that they are nothing but a bundle or collection of different perceptions, which succeed each other with inconceivable rapidity, and are in perpetual flux and movement. . . . The mind is a kind of theatre, where several perceptions successively make their appearance ; pass, repass, glide away, and mingle in an infinite variety of postures and situations."

In other words, when we introspect we do not come across states of mind owned by an Ego ; there is no timeless particular at the centre, but merely a succession of mental events which has the sort of unity of a swarm of bees. A similar nihilism was put forward by Hindu philosophers long before it appeared in the West : " What appears as self is but a bundle of ideas, emotions, and active tendencies, manifesting at a particular moment. The next moment they dissolve and new bundles determined by the preceding ones appear. The present thought is thus the only thinker. Apart from emotions, ideas, and active tendencies we cannot discover any separate self or soul." (*Indian Philosophy*, Dasgupta.)

Causality and Induction

It was one thing to shock metaphysicians and theologians ; but Hume also shocked the scientists. For what sort of science can be made out of bundles of momentary sense-impressions ? In the eighteenth century it was generally believed that by inductive reasoning it is possible to obtain universal laws. Newton had extended the reign of law from solar system to the entire physical cosmos. His laws of motion applied to all particles of matter whatsoever. He certainly did not regard the Law of Gravity as a mere description of observed phenomena ; but if knowledge is confined to the present moment, not even a descriptive law is possible.

Hume reverses the ancient complaint that our senses deceive us. We are deceived, he claims, not by our senses but by the interpretations we put on them. " If we reason *a priori*," writes Hume, " anything may appear able to produce anything. The falling of a pebble may, for aught we know, extinguish the sun, or the wish of a man may control the planets in their orbits." And so to find out what in fact produces a particular effect we must observe what happens. But how can mere observation tell us that what has happened will always continue to happen ? Unless we desert empiricism and take to metaphysics, all we can say is that we *expect* certain things to happen.

Our belief in the uniformity of nature is, therefore, no more than a feeling of expectation, based on custom, that the future will continue to conform to the past. The whole edifice of science rests on this feeling. We must, of course, trust our feelings in daily life ; for practical affairs it is enough that a thing should be probable. But *believing* is not the same as *knowing*.

" The mind never perceives any real connection among distinct existences," says Hume. So that when he regards " existences " objectively he cannot discover any necessary relation. But without some necessary relation, without causation, what ground is there for even trying to regard " existences " as objective ? And if they are not objective how can we hope to find causes, " since they are not in the mind " ? Causation alone can lead us to objects " which we do not see or feel."

He is well aware that to search for causes as the ground of objectivity is inconsistent with his view " that all our distinct perceptions are distinct existences," for that must end in Berkeley's Idealism. He confesses quite frankly that he cannot render these two principles consistent, " nor is it in my power to renounce either of them." But, having carefully bandaged his eyes, it is idle to look for an external world. Having assumed that every impression is discrete, it is useless to search for necessary connections.

At times he tries to mitigate his scepticism. " I have never defended the absurd proposition that a thing could come into being without cause," he says in one of his letters ; " all I maintained was only that our certainty of the falsehood of this proposition arises neither from intuition nor demonstration, but from another source." He could not consistently propound a Law of Association of Ideas, or his ethical theories, or write history, without employing the idea of causation ; but he was more consistent than most philosophers, and nowhere does he appeal to God to extricate him from his difficulties.

Hume was certainly two centuries ahead of his critics. They little dreamed that the time was coming when it would be possible to say that " in advanced sciences, such as gravitational astronomy, the word ' cause ' never occurs," or that " the reason why physics has ceased to look for causes is that, in fact, there are no such things " (*Mysticism and Logic*, by Bertrand Russell). Hume would not have felt such melancholy, or been so " affrighted and confounded with that forlorn solitude in which I am placed in my philosophy," if he could have foreseen that a powerful school would arise on the foundations that he laid and teach that induction was merely a practical rule of behaviour without any logical basis, that there was no *a priori* method of inferring the unknown from the known, and that the laws of thought were tautologies.

He realized, far more deeply than any of his contemporaries, what the break with Rationalism implied. After Hume the most urgent problem of philosophy was this : If knowledge is restricted to immediate experience, how can we justify the world that reason constructs ? The empirical method seemed to have severed the connection between these two worlds. How could that connection be restored without a return to metaphysics ?

Empiricism, which started with such bland confidence, suddenly seemed to end in a barren scepticism which not only affronted common sense, but made the science of the day seem impossible. Philosophers have never been very tender with common sense, but to destroy the basis of science is another matter. How is science possible if there is no justification for the belief in causality and induction? And if mathematics is dissevered from the real world, how is it that mathematics can be successfully applied to real problems?

USEFUL REFERENCES

Berkeley's Immaterialism, by A. A. Luce (1946), is a good introduction, but Berkeley and Hume themselves can be read with enjoyment.
The Principles of Human Knowledge, by George Berkeley; 1710.
Three Dialogues Between Hylas and Philonous, by George Berkeley; 1713.
A Treatise of Human Nature, by David Hume; 1739.
An Inquiry Concerning Human Understanding, by David Hume; 1748.

CHAPTER SEVEN

The Kantian Compromise

WHEN we look away from the details of the great struggle between the Rationalists and the Empiricists we can see that the fight was not really about the issues that seemed most important to the contestants. It was not about the reality of the external world or the soul or God. Whether there were one or two or an infinite number of substances was a side-issue. Whether to abandon the whole idea of a material substratum was not the really fundamental question. Out of all the din and confusion there emerged a re-statement of that very old riddle—What is a universal?

This may seem a dull business compared with the achievements that the philosophers claimed. Berkeley had " annihilated all that's made to a green thought in a green shade." Hume had destroyed the mind itself and blown up the foundations on which science rested. Such desperate deeds make good reading, but the solid gains that accrued from all this intense intellectual activity were less sensational. Perhaps the most important advance was the emergence of the problem of universals in a new dress. The question became, What relation does a concept bear to a percept?

If we can answer that question satisfactorily much else falls into place. We shall then know whether we are justified in talking about an external world, about causes, substance, matter, and mind. For on the correct solution of this problem depends the possibility of any real knowledge. And whether we can solve it or not, at least we are not wasting our time on irrelevancies.

The Failure of Rationalism

Kant believed that he had solved it. Before examining the answer he proposed, let us take a brief, backward glance at some of the earlier attempts. We shall then notice that the first formulations of the problem were more concerned with the reality of universals than with the manner in which they were connected with percepts. The fact that relations were also universals was usually ignored. Before Leibniz no one gave much serious consideration to the possibility that space might be a relation. It evidently required a great effort to distinguish between abstracta—such as numbers—and existents, such as tables and chairs; between sensuous concepts and non-sensuous concepts.

Plato held that concepts were real. They existed independently of objects. Knowledge derived from the senses was vague and confused; we were watching the play of shadows cast on a wall by unseen actors. Reason, however, gave us a backstage view.

Aristotle rejected the independent reality of concepts; but he thought that they were genuine ingredients of reality. They were not mere names. It would seem that by logical abstraction we can ignore what is accidental in a thing and discover its inmost essence. But peel off all qualities and you come to bare, undifferentiated being. By adding qualities you can arrive at any particular object. It might seem to follow that new knowledge about the real world can be obtained by reasoning.

Descartes held that concepts are innate. They are given to us, as part of the materials of knowledge. A valid concept can be recognized when it is a " clear and distinct " idea. Without such concepts—matter, motion, cause, etc.—how is it possible to frame scientific laws? And what can we mean by knowledge, urged Spinoza, if reason cannot discover real connections?

Such, in brief, was the rationalist approach. There are many variations, but there is general agreement that the mind does not manufacture concepts out of sense-data. We have to apply concepts to percepts in order to obtain knowledge. Rationalists held that it would be truer to say that a material object is a bundle of concepts than that a concept is a bundle of sense-data. The strongest argument in the Rationalist armoury was that to deny the reality of concepts is to deny the very possibility of knowledge.

Historically, however, the development of Rationalism came perilously close to denying the possibility of knowledge. The paradox, as I have already tried to show, arose out of a logic that required every proposition to have a metaphysical subject. This leads to the conclusion that there can be only one subject, strictly speaking—the Cosmos, the Absolute, or God. And that being the case, finite minds merely have a knowledge of certain aspects of the universe, so fragmentary that it is not far removed from illusion. By contrasting mere appearance with an ungraspable total reality, this type of metaphysics fell far short of its early promise. It ended on a note of scepticism which could be relieved only by mystical aids.

The Failure of Empiricism

The scepticism of the empiricists, however, could obtain no such relief. It entailed the following doctrines : (1) That concepts are mainly symbols which combine a cluster of percepts ; (2) that the sole objects of knowledge are percepts ; (3) that there are no necessary relations between percepts.

At first sight this looks as though the empiricist has swept away a lot of useless metaphysical lumber and got down to hard facts. But will it work ? Locke tried to make it work, at the cost of consistency, by retaining the metaphysical idea of substance. Berkeley had to introduce a sort of concept which he called " notion," but never properly explained. Hume resorted to no such doubtful expedients, but even he could not make the scheme work.

He showed that some concepts could be derived from percepts—sensuous concepts such as horse, mountain, etc. He tried, with much less success, to construct space and time in this way. He failed with non-sensuous concepts and jettisoned them. But what he did not notice was that even his apparent success with sensuous concepts made use of an idea that cannot be obtained direct from observation.

A horse and a mountain are general terms ; but if they are obtained by noting resemblances between particular horses and mountains, why is it that *some* similarities are selected and others rejected ? How is it possible to order particulars according to a principle of similarity, unless that principle is known in advance ? How can you arrange a Bridge hand if you do not know the rules of Bridge ?

This is a very subtle point, and Hume might protest that the mind does no arranging—it is purely passive, and the particular impressions arrange themselves mechanically into complexes according to the Law of Association. But if knowledge is confined to an immediate presentation, how can you avoid what has been called " the solipsism of the present moment " ? What right have you to trust memory and frame a law ?

Standing on the shoulders of those who have gone before us, we can see to-day how some of the difficulties with which the empiricists grappled might have been avoided. A neo-Kantian, Cassirer, writes : " Memory traces, arising equally with present images, are not *recognised* as similar elements. The foundation of all abstraction is an act of identification. A function is ascribed to thought : viz., to relate a present to a past content and comprehend the two as in some respect identical. This synthesis possesses no immediate sensible correlate in the content compared. The psychology of abstraction must first postulate that perceptions can be ordered for logical consideration into ' series of similars.' The transition from member to member presupposes a principle according to which it takes place and the form of dependence between each member and the succeeding one is determined. Thus the construction of concepts is connected with the formation of a series."

Similarity does not appear as an element in sensation, side by side with colours and sounds, pressure and touch. Before we can make use of similarity we must first gain a point of view from which things can be compared, and this is not given in immediate experience.   We need not construct concepts solely according to similarity ; we could have a series exposing differences, ordered according to equality or inequality, number and magnitude, causal dependence, etc.

Again, as Prof. C. I. Lewis has pointed out in *Mind and the World Order*, the empirical object denoted by a concept is never what is momentarily given, but is some temporarily extended pattern of actual and possible experiences.   We see tables and chairs, not patches of colour.   " In experience the mind is confronted with the chaos of the given.   In the interests of adaptation and control it seeks to discover within or impose upon this chaos some kind of stable order, through which distinguishable items may become the signs of future possibilities."   These ordered patterns are concepts, and must be determined in advance of the experience to which they apply.   Until the criteria of interpretation are fixed, no experiences can be the sign of anything.

These modern authors show, in different degrees, the influence of Kant.   The passages I have cited help to show the nature of the problem which the empiricists brought to light and which Kant tried to solve.

The Age of Professors

Immanuel Kant (1724–1804) was born in Koenigsberg, and his father was a saddler of Scottish descent.   There is very little to say about his life, for he seldom left his native city and never the province.   He led a quiet, studious, strictly methodical existence.   He did not marry and no scandals attach to him.   He was the type of unworldly scholar to which popular imagination seems to expect philosophers to conform.   With the appearance of Kant the amateurs retire from the scene for a time and the professionals take charge.

Bacon was a lawyer, Hobbes a secretary and tutor, Spinoza an optician, Leibniz a librarian and diplomat, Locke a doctor and Government official, Berkeley a bishop, Hume a librarian and historian.   These men were not academic recluses.   If their speculations were unlikely to meet with the approval of the authorities, they could refrain from publishing books without endangering their livelihood.

They were not expected to produce monumental treatises. They had a breadth of culture that made them sensitive to literary style. They are nearly all readable and quotable.

When philosophy fell into the hands of German professors, however, it became unreadable and almost unintelligible. It developed a new jargon, even more complicated, and far more uncouth, than the technicalities of the classical and medieval schools. Kant is not so bad in this respect as his successors, notably Hegel. And he certainly put up a strong resistance to the pressure to please the authorities.

His earlier writings were mainly about physical problems. He read the English empiricists and was deeply perturbed by Hume's scepticism. Then he was influenced in the direction of Rationalism by Leibniz's *Nouveaux Essais*, published in 1765. He wavered between Empiricism and Rationalism, and his final position, stated in the *Critique of Pure Reason* (1781) is a compromise. The *Critique of Practical Reason* appeared in 1788, and the *Critique of Judgment* in 1790.

Kant was keenly conscious that Hume had precipitated a crisis in philosophy. He declared that Hume had awakened him from his dogmatic slumbers and he saw that the war between the Rationalists and the Empiricists had ended in stalemate. No further progress could be made until a more satisfactory account was given of those concepts that appear to be independent of experience. They must either be dropped, and all hope of real knowledge abandoned, or else they must be justified.

Before examining in detail Kant's theory, let us look at the terminology he employs. It is difficult, and he does not always use words consistently. Moreover, he derives some of the terms from a psychology now happily obsolete. He divides the mind into two parts : the lower is the sensuous part ; the higher, the understanding. The senses are acted on by some outside stimulus. As a result there appear in the consciousness

G

certain representations. These are connected, like beads on a string. The higher part of the mind has a double task. It pronounces judgments and makes inferences.

For convenience we will restrict the term "understanding" to what Kant calls "the faculty of judging." We will use "reason" to mean "the faculty of inference." The power to make judgments requires the power to create concepts. So does the power to make inferences. But Kant draws an important distinction between two sorts of concepts. Those which are used in judging by the understanding are pure concepts. They could also be called connective concepts, because they are used to connect.

The concepts of the faculty of inference are called by Kant the Ideas of Reason. They do not link up representations so that the mind gets a unified pattern out of the brute facts of the given. They are largely used to state problems, and they are non-empirical. The meaning of this will become plainer as we proceed.

Now we come to another basic but most unfortunately chosen term—"intuition." Our ordinary associations with this word must be put out of mind. By intuition (*Anschauung* —literally, "view") Kant means a sort of knowledge we get on direct acquaintance. It is a sort of perception, though not with the naked eye.

Suppose we are in a dark, curtained room and can see nothing. The curtains are flung back and we get a view of the landscape outside. But the window-panes are made of a peculiar glass. It distorts the landscape, but it is unbreakable glass and the room is locked, so that we can never go outside and measure the distortion. This must not be confused with illusion; we may be deceived, but we are not deluded, as a lunatic would be if there was no landscape but only a brick wall outside.

The intuitions (views) of the senses have a real content. They give us the objects which form the raw material of knowledge. It would be a great mistake to suppose that it even occurred to Kant to doubt the reality of an external landscape. But he insisted that we see it through windows—the windows of the mind. A better analogy would be those lenses which are sometimes fitted to the eyeballs to take the place of spectacles—but we must regard it as being impossible to remove them.

Without these lenses we should not get the sort of distortion that we do. We should not see things spread out in space. Both space and time are forms of intuition: space the form of a kind of outer sense, which makes it possible for objects to seem external to us; time of a kind of inner sense, which gives us the order of succession. They are logically prior to percepts. They are the conditions under which we experience. They are not abstracted from experience and they are not " generic " terms. To emphasize this, Kant does not call them concepts, but *forms*.

No knowledge can be obtained by merely staring at a landscape. To know you must think—you must pass judgment. Intuitions are particulars (like simple ideas); to connect them so that we can pass judgment, we form concepts. The procedure is as follows: raw sensations are ordered in space and time by the mind; they become particular intuitions, but they still lack the connections which give us a unified knowledge. A synthesizing activity is needed, so that we can think as well as merely perceive. And this calls for more than empirical concepts—more than generic terms, such as horse and man. We cannot think without pure non-sensuous concepts. To these Kant gives the name *categories*.

The Meaning of the "A Priori"

Kant supplies a formidable array of technical terms, but we need not bother about all of them. In the previous chapter I illustrated the difference between analytic and synthetic concepts. The latter are used when we express facts of experience. But are not mathematical propositions also facts?

To show how universally true propositions are possible about experience, Kant must show how we can make statements about facts that are not analytic—the predicate of which is not hidden in the subject. Such propositions must be independent of experience, but must nevertheless refer to experience.

Kant calls them *a priori* synthetic judgments, and he gives as an example $5 + 7 = 12$. We know that that will always be true ; whereas " all crows are black " is an *a posteriori* judgment and can be upset by the discovery of a white crow.

If synthetic *a priori* judgments are justifiable, the connection between the world of ideas and the world of fact severed by Hume can be restored.

Kant's solution is a masterpiece of compromise. He dismisses, as an over-simplification, the view that all concepts are derived from sense-experience. The categories are not mere names for bundles of percepts ; they are too abstract for that. Neither are they obtained by logical abstraction. The categories are the common language of mankind, the way we *must* talk when we pass judgments, the way we simply cannot help thinking. There is no choice about it.

What is given to us in sensation is automatically made into a spatial object by the mind. It starts as a particular. But to *think* about these particulars is to unify them, to judge them. And the mind is so constituted that certain words *must* be used. Different human languages may employ different signs, but they have the same meanings. The structure of thought is the same for all men. The categories exhibit the structure of thought. If there are angels, they may think about the world in wholly different terms ; if so, we could not hold intelligible conversation with an angel.

The structure of thought is logically prior to experience. Two common misunderstandings of Kant may arise at this point. There is the crude objection that the psychology of children shows that a knowledge of space and time is acquired by degrees. This does not upset Kant's theory. He would reply that what is learned is about ourselves, not about things outside us. That is what the difference between logical and psychological priority amounts to.

The second mistake that can easily be made is to regard space and time themselves as categories. This is to ignore Kant's faculty-psychology. Space is at a lower level than non-sensuous concepts. It is the form that determines how sensations become objects. Extension is the form of sensation—a blank cheque to be filled in with colours, sounds, tastes, and smells. Extension is the pre-requisite of an object. It need not be red or smell like a rose. It could be of some other colour and smell like an onion. But however it smells it must be spatial. Empirical or sensuous concepts, such as red and scent, are not universal and necessary. Space is different; it is the cheque to be filled in, the prior form which the mind provides, and without which percepts could not arise. The same holds good of time.

This is Kant's solution, in a nutshell. The mind is neither passive, as the empiricists taught, nor endowed with innate ideas that enable it to discover the nature of a reality beyond the senses. The mind is active and it creates its own world. Space, time, and the categories of the mind are pure forms, prior to experience and contributed by the mind itself. Given an external stimulus, these pure forms fashion for us the phenomenal world. They do not fashion it out of nothing, but in the nature of things our knowledge is limited to what can be expressed in the basic, conceptual language. It is, however, genuine knowledge about phenomena.

Kant claimed that he had made objects conform to the mind, whereas previous philosophers had made mind conform to objects. He likened this achievement to that of Copernicus. It seemed to him that it made all other philosophers look like flat-earthers. He believed that he had settled the great controversy between empiricists and Rationalists. Both schools were wrong. The mind was active, and the conditions of experience set a limit to knowledge without making knowledge impossible.

Categories of the Understanding

The theory of categories is perhaps the most difficult and most easily misunderstood part of Kant's philosophy. Let us look at it more closely.

The categories make thinking, as distinct from sensing, possible. How can we discover what these categories are?

How many pure concepts are essential to enable us to pass judgments ?   When we think of the bewilderingly large number of words we use it seems almost impossible to select just those basic ideas that are indispensable to thought and common to all mankind.   Kant's solution is ingenious, though it places great trust in traditional logic.   He derives the categories from the traditional forms of judgment.

The four classes of judgment involve twelve basic ideas which are the presuppositions of thought.   Such schematization is out of fashion to-day ; and it was not long after Kant that the whole procedure was seen to contain a contradition fatal to one of his main doctrines.   But let us first look at the list of judgments and categories.   The types of judgment are as follows :—

Quantitative.	Universal, Particular, Singular.
Qualitative.	Affirmative, Negative, Infinite.
Relational.	Categorical, Hypothetical, Disjunctive.
Modal.	Problematic, Assertoric, Apodeictic.

The corresponding categories are as follows :—

Quantitative.	Totality, Plurality, Unity.
Qualitative.	Reality, Negation, Limitation.
Relational.	Substance and Accident, Cause and Effect, Reciprocity.
Modal.	Possibility and Impossibility, Existence and Non-Existence, Necessity and Contingency.

If I say " A rose is red," I mean that a spatio-temporal object exists and has the empirical quality of redness.   There is an ambiguity about " is," but for the moment we will ignore it. Clearly the above proposition would be unintelligible if it did not refer to a percept and an empirical concept and presuppose the more abstract idea of reality or existence.   Now, Kant's point is that percepts would be unintelligible without categories.

The categories (if they are necessary and *a priori*) must be derived from purely formal propositions.   " A rose is red " has the logical form " S is P."   Another form would be " Some S is P."   Let us consider what ideas are involved in the latter.

To begin with it refers to " *some* S," and so it is neither universal nor singular.   There remains only the concept particular out of the three quantitative types of judgment.   And since there is more than one S, but not " *all* S," we must take from the above table the category of plurality.   Various types of propositions have the various concepts embedded in them.

The result is a sort of Realism within an Idealism.   The categories make real knowledge possible ; but they do not apply to whatever lies beyond the ideal constructions of the mind. Kant calls what lies beyond, " things-in-themselves," in contrast to things as they appear to us : Noumena as opposed to Phenomena.

Kant often fails to make his meaning plain.   Different sections of the *Critique of Pure Reason* were composed at different times, and some of the statements clash.   But he seems to distinguish between phenomena and our mind-pictures of phenomena.   Knowledge of phenomena must not be confined to bare perception.   The fact that the earth goes round the sun is a part of our genuine knowledge of phenomena ; but in our mind-pictures it is the sun and not the earth that moves.

Obviously Kant is saying something that it is not easy to express in words.   He is trying to demonstrate that there is an element of construction and interpretation in all our knowledge. Bare, unrelated sense-impressions are not the field of consciousness—they could not be known.   But neither can we know what causes them.

The Unknowable

The concept " reality " is listed (see above) as one of the categories of thought.   All those twelve categories are forms which we impress—on what ?   On things-in-themselves ?   Are the latter not *real*, then ?   Consult the list again.   Cause and effect are due to the spectacles through which we must look. We are constitutionally compelled to order phenomena causally. But does not Kant regard noumena as though they were causes of phenomena ?   Does he not, as Whitehead complains,

" bifurcate nature into real and apparent," so that the familiar world is merely the outcome for us of an inscrutable world which we can never truly know ? Existence is another category—then cannot we say the noumena *exist* ? In short, what can we possibly assert of things-in-themselves if we do not employ any of the twelve categories ?

It may be objected—" Of course you cannot assert anything without using those pure concepts." That is what Kant means by calling them *a priori*. You cannot *speak* about " the unknowable." The empiricist would reply that the unknowable now begins to resemble the God of certain mystics, of which nothing can be asserted. It is not real ; it does not exist. It is not cause or substance. It is neither quantity, quality, nor relation. To speak of it as the ground, and of appearance as the consequent, may indicate what Kant had in mind, but is not permissible. We cannot validly speak of the unknowable ; and so it is for Kant to show how we can even *name* it.

There are few open defenders of the unknowable to-day. The concept appears self-contradictory and offends the instinct of logical economy. No doubt our knowledge of appearances is a sort of *knowledge* ; but we are forever left in ignorance of the reality assumed to lie beyond appearances. The question naturally occurs to the modern reader : Does not science offer a glimpse of this reality ? Modern physics, for example, dispenses with some, at least, of the categories. It can manage at a pinch without causation and substance. Instead of space and time, Relativity employs intervals. The categories may be necessities at a certain level of thinking ; but all of them are not essential in the most advanced field of science.

This sort of difficulty did not exist for Leibniz, whose view that the material world was an ideal representation certainly influenced Kant. Leibniz could allow for different levels of apperception ; and in any case he held that space and time were relational, though relations were unreal.

Kant cut off any retreat into metaphysics by denying we could have positive knowledge of noumena by an intellectual equivalent of sensuous perception. If intuition could reveal the inner nature of reality, he would have been spared a contradiction—but what would have become of his rejection of metaphysics ? All he could do was to say that we can think of the unknowable as a limit. But Hegel objected that to be aware of a limit it is necessary to know what lies beyond it. If, indeed, there is an absolute limit to knowledge, how can we become aware of the fact ? How can we know that we have reached the last wall unless we can look over the top ?

The Ideas of Reason

By inclination Kant was a metaphysician. But his analysis of mind committed him to denying that new existents could be discovered solely by connecting categories. What, then, of God, the soul, the freedom of the will, all of which have a prominent place in his system ?

He faces this frankly. We cannot prove the existence of God, the immortality of the soul, or the freedom of the will. We could attempt to do so only by abandoning the empirical foundation in favour of deductive rationalism. The modern Positivist would call these things pseudo-concepts. Kant regards them as ideas of the reasoning faculty. There is, however, no intuitive perception, no direct acquaintance possible for reason. It uses its ideas to state problems or construct hypotheses. Its ideas do not have an ontological object. They are not windows that open on reality.

When we overlook this we are guilty of an abuse of language. If we forget our limitations and behave like the metaphysicians we end up with antinomies—propositions of which the opposite is neither more nor less acceptable.

For example, there are excellent logical proofs that the world began in time and is limited in space. But there are equally good logical reasons for asserting that the world never had a beginning and that space is infinite.

We can " prove," on paper, that God exists and that the soul is immortal. We can also " prove," on paper, that God does not exist and that the soul is not immortal. Eminent philosophers have advanced all these " proofs." They are all right and they are all wrong. To put forward such proofs is to use logic in an invalid way. The propositions are formally correct but existentially empty. It is all a game with words.

Kant unquestionably smashed to pieces all the classical proofs of the existence of God. Since his day no reputable philosopher outside the Catholic Church has dared to revive them. We cannot possibly demonstrate God's existence from the fact that we can *think* of his existence, Kant says; and he reaffirms Aristotle's view that existence is not a predicate. We do not enrich a concept by adding *being*. A hundred real dollars do not contain a penny more than a hundred conceived dollars. All existential propositions are synthetic. We should express this differently nowadays, but it seems clear enough that the confusion is partly due to the grammatical ambiguity of the verb to-be.

It is a pity that Kant did not fully exploit this doctrine. However, his attack on speculative theology caused considerable dismay at first. Would it result in Atheism? The dialectical performance was watched by a breathless audience, as though he were a conjurer, sawing through the lady in the box. But there need have been no anxiety. Just as the conjurer takes the curtain with the lady completely restored, so Kant gives back with his left hand all that his right hand has taken away.

" I was obliged to destroy knowledge in order to make room for faith," he confesses. We cannot prove by logic the existence of God, the freedom of the will, or the immortality of the soul. But when we turn from Pure Reason to Practical Reason it happily becomes clear that we must assume these things. Philosophy does not merely answer the question, What do we know? It must answer the more practical questions, What ought we to do? What may we hope?

" After we have satisfied ourselves of the vanity of all the ambitious attempts of reason to fly beyond the bound of experience, enough remains of practical value to content us. It is true that no one may boast that he *knows* that God and a future life exist; for if he possesses such knowledge he is just the man for whom I have long been seeking. All knowledge (touching an object of mere reason) can be communicated, and therefore I might hope to see my own knowledge increased to this prodigious extent by his instruction. No, our conviction in these matters is not *logical*, but *moral* certainty ; and, inasmuch as it rests upon subjective grounds (of moral disposition), I must not even say *it is* morally certain that there is a God, and so on, but *I am* morally certain, and so on. That is to say, the belief in a God and in another world is so interwoven with my moral nature that the former can no more vanish than the latter can ever be torn from me."

The conviction that there is a moral law justifies us in assuming the existence of God. Philosophers may doubt the reality of matter and question physical laws, but to doubt that right is right and wrong is wrong seemed to Kant quite intolerable.

Reason must supply a meaning to the word *ought* ; and such a meaning shows that the moral law must be formal—i.e., not a recommendation to practise specific virtues—and apply in all circumstances. The general form of the law is a command : " Act only on that maxim whereby thou canst at the same time will that it should become a universal law."

There is a Calvinistic flavour about all this and also a hint of the Prussian barrack square. Kant held that if society were on the point of dissolution, the last act of the Government must be to see that all condemned felons are hanged. It follows that if the Gestapo come after your mother you must not tell a lie even to save her from being tortured in a concentration camp.

The Consequences of Kant

Summing up Kant's contribution, Professor A. C. Ewing writes : " That all propositions are partly *a priori* and partly empirical, that the mind exercises a far greater organizing function even in sense-perception than had been realized hitherto so that perception is impossible without conception and we are acquainted with nothing which is merely given without interpretation, that the unity of the self is not that of an unchanging, simple substance but is to be found in the functional unity of experience, that the knowing self and its

objects are correlative so that there can be no self without
objects and no objects without an experiencing self, that physical objects are best regarded as systems of sense-data unified by
general laws common to all human experience, are doctrines
which, whether right or wrong, clearly emerge . . . and have
exercised a great influence ever since." (Section on Kantianism in *Twentieth-Century Philosophy*.)

The chief stumbling-block to Kant's successors was the
thing-in-itself. It was obviously unsatisfactory. Fichte rejected it, and so did Hegel, but not because it was "metaphysical." It seemed to Hegel that the empiricists had had
their innings, but they had failed to explain how genuine
knowledge was possible—how concepts could disclose necessary
and universal relations. He concluded that philosophy had
taken the wrong road and that a return to metaphysics was the
only solution.

Hegel accepted part of Kant's analysis of concepts. He
regarded their division into sensuous and non-sensuous, and
the use of *a priori* categories, as a considerable advance on the
Platonic theory of Ideas, in which no classification was attempted. But he would not admit that there was any limit to
knowledge.

He took one of the most fiercely debated steps in the history
of philosophy. He dropped the thing-in-itself and phenomena,
but he retained the categories. They were not subjective forms
of experience, as Kant had taught ; they were as objective as
Plato believed his Ideas to be.

And so began the "unearthly ballet of bloodless categories,"
against which Bradley inveighed. A new horizon was instantly
disclosed. Whether it gives us mirage or reality is still dis-
puted. It certainly provides the excitement of a wholly fresh
perspective. How to make it intelligible I do not know.
Hegel's own writings seem to me almost completely incompre-
hensible, and I must state frankly that I have leaned heavily on
his interpreters—always bearing in mind his own complaint
that only one man had understood him and that even he had
got most of it wrong.

Useful References

Kant, by A. D. Lindsay; 1934.
A Commentary to Kant's Critique of Pure Reason, by Norman Kemp Smith; 1923.
Kant's Metaphysic of Experience, by H. J. Paton; 1936.
A Study of Kant, by James Ward; 1902.
The Critique of Pure Reason, by Immanuel Kant; 1781–87.
The Critique of Practical Reason, by Immanuel Kant; 1788.
The Critique of Judgment, by Immanuel Kant; 1789–93.

CHAPTER EIGHT

The Return to Metaphysics

THIS book is designed for the reader with little or no knowledge of philosophy. I am afraid that he will now find the going pretty heavy. As I have already stressed, we are no longer dealing with the speculations of shrewd men-of-the-world who wrote for a cultivated but non-specialist public. We have reached an awkward period when professors wrote for other professors.

It would be idle to pretend that philosophy is an easy subject. We may be quite sure that any system of philosophy that calls for no effort to understand it is false. The entire framework of human speculation is not likely to be simpler to grasp than its parts. Modern physical theories are not easy, and they deal only with one aspect of the problem that confronts the philosopher.

In a sense it is a sign of progress when a subject becomes difficult. Thus it is easier to read a text-book of psychology than of physics, not because the problems of psychology are simpler—on the contrary—but because we do not know so many answers.

Looking back from the point where Hegel took over from Kant, Fichte, and Schelling, we can see that in the seventeenth century there was an interruption in the main stream of inquiry. Before Locke, philosophers were concerned to find an *explanation* of the universe. Suddenly the whole of their procedure was challenged. Suppose there were limits to what the human mind could know? Suppose the quest for an explanation was destined to founder on the rocks of human fallibility?

A new school arose emphasizing the limitations of the mind. The faith of the traditional philosophers in logic as an instrument for discovering new truths was shaken. Nor could intuition come to the rescue; that road was also blocked. Experience was the corner-stone of the new school. What lay outside possible experience was regarded as an unknown, and even unknowable, territory that the philosopher must not try to penetrate.

Accordingly it was held that metaphysics was a waste of time, a mere fiddling with words. It followed that to look for a general explanation—to ask *why* grass was green, or *why* the earth went round the sun—was futile. You could hold that grass was green because God made it so, but why he should not make white grass was an inscrutable mystery. The scientists could answer *how*, but when the philosopher was asked *why* he must remain dumb.

What Constitutes an Explanation

Hegel (1770–1831) was profoundly dissatisfied with this situation. He was prepared to admit that the interruption of metaphysical inquiry had cleared the air, but he sought some escape from the sceptical impasse to which even Kant had been driven.

There must surely be some explanation of the universe—or of the ordering of experience which passes for knowledge. It is all very well to say that it is impossible to predict the future, but we do so in fact with success. It is all very well to conclude from Hume that there is no *reason* why water in a kettle should not freeze; in fact, if the kettle is put on a fire the water boils. So, obviously there are laws of nature. Obviously we are not faced by pure chaos. And if Kant's unknowable thing-in-itself is a contradiction in terms, if we cannot sensibly assert that reality is unknowable, the Maginot line is pierced—there are not limits to knowledge and all reality is knowable. Even the explanation can be known.

But what is meant by an explanation? According to Hegel it is something seen to follow of necessity from something else, just as the conclusion of a syllogism follows from the premises. This is not the same relation as cause and effect. Hume is right on that point. The boiling of water does not follow from the application of heat as a logical conclusion follows from a premise. Nor will it help if we trace back the chain of causes to a First Cause. We shall then have to explain the First Cause.

The search for an explanation must not come to rest on anything arbitrary. What is required is not a cause, but the reason for a cause—a reason of which the world is a consequent. If we could indeed find such a reason, everything that happens would be a consequence of it and would be deducible from it. We should not have to bother about observing and experimenting—we could sit down and deduce the nature of the world.

Mere empirical facts tell us little. We can see that oil burns and ice melts, but we can make no deductions from such bare isolated facts. If the whole universe is nothing but an aggregate of isolated facts—individual atoms, simple ideas, sense-impressions, call them what you will—the empiricists are perfectly correct, and no reason can be discovered for the order of Nature. We must then take refuge in a vague feeling that some beliefs are more probable than others ; or, like Hume, we must abandon the quest as hopeless, dismiss philosophy as an esoteric pastime, and turn with relief to backgammon.

But if, on the other hand, the universe is not a mere aggregate, but an organic whole, every part of it will send out some thread of connection with every other part. This means a return to Spinoza's vision of a single reality, every individual aspect of which is what it is because of the character of the whole. Such a reality is rational, because reason can discover universal laws which express the character of the parts and therefore yield genuine knowledge as opposed to " the twilight of probability."

Spinoza held that the universe was one substance—which he called God—with an infinite number of attributes. He held that we knew only two of these attributes, thought and extension —beyond these stretch an infinite unknowable. Hegel accepted Spinoza's Monism, but he rejected the limit placed on what could be known. If reason can find an explanation there is no such limit.

Reality is Thought, Not Matter

What, then, is the solution ?   The first step is to assume that the total reality is one ; but Hegel believed that " substance " was not primitive enough to be taken as the starting-point of deduction.   The " stuff " of the world is not matter and mind, still less matter alone.   The world-stuff is entirely mental—as mental (or spiritual) as Berkeley believed.   It consists of thought—and *nothing but thought*.

So far Hegel makes no startling innovation.   He seems, on the face of it, to offer a solution rather like Berkeley's Immaterialism.   He rejects not only the logically indefensible substratum that worried Locke, but the thing-in-itself which was the unsatisfactory feature of Kant's scheme.   But it would be a bad blunder to suppose that by " thought " Hegel meant anything resembling the " ideas " of the English empiricists. By thought he meant what Plato called " ideas " and Aristotle " universals."   From Plato he took the suggestion that the thoughts of which the world is made are objective, and not, as Kant taught, subjective.   And so, *the* world, according to Hegel, (and not merely *our* private worlds,) is quite literally composed of concepts.   Apart from concepts there is nothing.

But he departed from Plato and supported Kant in distinguishing two kinds of concepts, sensuous and non-sensuous. The reason of the world, according to Hegel, lies in the nature of pure concepts.   From these concepts (which are like Kant's twelve categories but more numerous) he claimed to be able to deduce every feature of the world, even the course of its history and the development of social institutions.   Such a claim sounds fantastic, but we must remember this : *if* the trick can be done, Hegel has succeeded in discovering the explanation that philosophers before him had sought as ardently as the alchemists searched for the secret of making gold.   For *if* reality does consist of concepts, and of nothing else, the world must flow from their nature as necessarily as a conclusion from premises.   Indeed, there is no longer logic on one side, shut off by an impenetrable wall from fact.   There is no longer the

H

old baffling contradiction between the world of reason and the world of everyday appearances.   Fact and logic are identical if this is the case ; if " things " are congeries of thoughts, " things " are related in exactly the same way as logical terms. Indeed, Nature is composed of the same " material " as logic.

" I refute it thus ! " Dr. Johnson might say, once again kicking a stone.   But, once more, what does he refute ?   The qualities of hardness, greyness, coldness, etc., are not denied. These, however, are not " simple ideas."   They are not particulars.   They are universals.   A stone is merely a bundle of universals, according to Hegel.   Unified as a bundle it is an individual thing.   To say that it " exists " is to assert its individuality—its lack of universality.

This will be intelligible to those who have followed me in earlier chapters.   It amounts to saying that we know nothing of an object apart from the concepts that constitute it.   Indeed, there is nothing more to know.

Such concepts are sensuous, it may be objected.   What of Hegel's claim to deduce the stone from non-sensuous categories ?   Grant that hardness and greyness—the whole set of appearances of the stone—are universals and truly exist in a certain combination, how can such definite characteristics be deduced from non-sensuous concepts, such as totality, plurality, singularity, etc. ?   How can Hegel possibly maintain that such abstractions as these exist objectively ?

The answer to the last question is that Hegel does not hold that universals exist.   Well, then, it will be instantly retorted, if they do not exist how can they form the ground of the world, the reason from which nature flows as a consequent ?   The reply that Hegel gives has seemed to many of his critics mere word-spinning.   His answer is that pure concepts do not exist, but they are real ; whereas individual objects exist but are not real.   Sensuous concepts, being universals, are real, but they exist only as collections—they occupy a no-man's land sometimes called " subsistence."

The Universal Philosophy

" This sickening humbug ! " exclaimed Schopenhauer. He went on to describe Hegel as a " spiritless and tasteless charlatan . . . . We see with what tricks he was able to hold the learned world of Germany for thirty years." That Schopenhauer was personally jealous of Hegel's success can hardly be doubted ; but it is easy enough to see why Hegel should be regarded as a sophist. I do not think, however, that this harsh judgment can be accepted. I personally believe that Hegel failed in his central purpose ; but it was something worth attempting. His failure was a bigger achievement than most people's successes, despite its extravagances and occasional absurdities.

Hegel tried to find a way out of the sceptical impasse. He tried to show what the world must be like if it was susceptible of a rational explanation. If his solution had a paradoxical air, that was certainly nothing new. He made a heroic endeavour to abolish all arbitrary assumptions and justify the method of deductive metaphysics. His aim was to formulate a universal philosophy that embraced all the progress which he believed had been made by his predecessors.

As William Wallace puts it : " What Hegel proposes to give is no novel or special doctrine, but the universal philosophy which has passed on from age to age, here narrowed and there widened, but still essentially the same. It is conscious of its continuity and proud of its identity with the teachings of Plato and Aristotle."

Viewed in the light of such an endeavour, his solution was not so outrageous as so many people have found it. Let us look more carefully at the apparent word-play, remembering the trouble that earlier philosophers had had with such ideas as " change " and " existence."

It seemed evident to Parmenides, for example, that change was a contradiction in terms—for what is, is ; and what is not, is not. As Zeno had pointed out, at any given instant a moving arrow is stationary. What is the alternative to saying that our senses deceive us, that the everyday world is a kind of illusion, that reason must build up a world of its own in defiance of the senses ? We cannot trust mere appearance ; so we must either give up the search for connections between things-in-themselves or be content with phenomenal knowledge.

This inevitably raised the question of what we mean when we say that something " exists." Do appearances exist or should we restrict the word to the reality behind them ? Do numbers, infinitesimals, minus quantities exist ? If a physical object turns out to be a collection of universals, how can we deny that the universals we thus experience exist and yet affirm that some material substratum, which nobody can experience, really and truly exists ?

Much of the confusion, of course, is due to the fact that the verb to-be can be employed in many different senses. Hegel broke with the sort of logic which deduces one proposition from another. He tried to deduce one term from another. But to express this he had to use propositions, and so he appeared, like Spinoza, to treat every assertion as attributing in the last resort a characteristic to one truly existing subject—the whole Cosmos. He was then faced with the problem of how a bit of the cosmos (Hegel himself) could regard the sole subject (which was not himself) as an object. How much simpler is the task of the solipsist, who can regard himself as the sole subject !

The Real is the Rational

Before we become entangled in this problem let us consider the new terms Hegel required to express the situation that there are, so to speak, two worlds, appearance and reality. The world of tables and books, people and stars, is said to *exist*. But the world of the mathematician and the logician, of numbers, symbols, abstract ideas, plainly does not exist in the same sense. Yet it is not mere nothing—indeed, such concepts as zero and infinity apply to the existing world and are used by engineers for very practical purposes. So these concepts have *being*, but they do not have *existence*. They are real—how else could they be applied to the everyday world ? It follows that being and reality are words which do not mean the same as existence.

When we say something is real we can mean only that it is universal. A sensuous concept, redness, is universal; it is not any particular red object; it is what all red objects have in common. The still more abstract concept, colour (abstracted from all specific shades) is what all red, blue, yellow objects have in common. The even more abstract and non-sensuous concept, being, mere "isness," is also universal. It is real, though it is not dependent on any particular state of affairs. But the particular stone that Dr. Johnson kicked is neither universal nor independent of other things. And since to be universal is what Hegel means by being real, a particular stone is not real. Like the rest of the coloured, changing world, it is not real, in a metaphysical sense, but it certainly exists.

When universals come together and form an individual object, that process is the birth of an existent. Of course, universals must not be imagined as rushing from the abysses of space and settling down to form a stone. If it is asked, *where* are universals? the reply must be nowhere—and nowhen. They do not exist, but they are real logical elements. They are not the basic material out of which the world is fashioned. They are prior to particular things, but this is a purely logical priority, not a priority in time. Otherwise they would be causes of particular things instead of their reason.

A dim perception of Hegel's meaning will perhaps begin to dawn on those readers who have had the patience to persevere. Universals are thoughts. A material object is a pattern of thoughts. The whole universe is an organized procession of thoughts, like the content of consciousness. The movement follows a law and has a direction. And so the universe of concepts, as it externalizes itself, has a meaning and a purpose. It is not blind matter but spirit (thought).

Such a law, if it can be found, will be the ultimate reason; once it is understood, it will exhibit the necessity for every type of change. It will be the law governing change itself—the same law governing the passage from seed to flower, acorn to oak, nebula to solar system, primitive savagery to civilization, mental conflict to its resolution, logical premise to its conclusion. This law will show how one category can be deduced from another, how the universe is a genus which contains within itself differentiæ and species that can be discovered, once you have the clue. And Hegel believed he had found the clue, the master-secret—the *Dialectic*, as he calls it.

Subject and Object

For the moment let us postpone consideration of this dialectical law, which claims to show the manner in which the universe of thought develops. The development which appears to us as the phenomenal world, the evolution of nature and the course of human history, is not the whole story. We cannot comprehend, in its full richness, the whole story so long as we merely look at it from the outside. We can see only the surface-play, only aspects of the total reality. And when we are restricted to a partial view we inevitably encounter contradictions. They are resolved as we widen our outlook, though still new contradictions arise. Everything in the universe is related to everything else and is, in a sense, determined by everything else. Thus the constitution of the whole enters into every part.

A piece of a jig-saw puzzle owes its shape to the way it has been cut ; it may be said to owe its shape to the way the parts into which it must be fitted have been cut, if the whole thing was cut from a single sheet of paper. This analogy must not be pressed too far, because the universe is infinitely complex, and a jig-saw is not a coherent and necessary system. But obviously Hegel was faced by the difficulty inherent in Spinoza's universe : how can you really know anything without knowing everything ? Hegel reversed Spinoza's dictum that all determination is negation ; for Hegel all negation is determination.

This sounds, admittedly, like more word-play. What he means is that when we say that something is *not* we discover something else that *is*. To negate is to posit. And the progress of the dialectic—which we shall soon consider—would not be possible unless by negating, or denying, one concept we arrived at another. Thus Hegel continually speaks of "the portentous power of the negative."

The idea of bare *being* gives us the idea of *nothing*. Being, without any sort of determination, is the same as nothing—as Berkeley had protested about bare matter. Being and nothing are opposites, and yet they are identical. This opposition and unity gives rise to the idea of *becoming*. And so we get a third concept.

We start with the idea of bare, qualityless *being* ; we see that it involves the notion of not-being (*nothing*) ; and when we consider how the one concept seems to pass into the other we find ourselves led irresistibly to reconcile the contradiction in a fresh concept, *becoming*.

Parmenides had looked at these concepts in isolation. He saw the contradiction between being and not-being, which appeared when he analysed becoming, but the rules of formal logic drove him back like a tabu. The really objectionable contradiction is between propositions, not terms.

Hegel boldly challenged the rules. They were merely formal, he said, and plainly they could not be applied to a world that really changes. A non-propositional logic was therefore demanded if change was to be taken seriously—and it could apply only if its elements were the very stuff of experience, or of reality—to choose a more objective term. The categories do, indeed, participate in a cosmic ballet, and the new logic shows the musical score.

The Unity of Opposites

There are three important features in this novel conception : (*a*) the subject-object relation ; (*b*) logical abstraction ; and (*c*) the identity of opposites. It is easier to ridicule these novelties than to understand what Hegel was trying to say. He was, of course, trying to express something almost impossible to convey by ordinary speech. The " learned gibberish " for which he is so often condemned is the result of a giant intellect struggling with the limitations of language in an agonizing attempt to communicate his vision.

The essence of Idealism is that *being* always entails being for consciousness. Without a subject that knows there can be no object that is known. If there are no contents within consciousness, if there is a blank, how can we speak of a conscious subject ? It would not be conscious of anything ; indeed, it would not be anything.

Similarly, if there is no subject, how can there be an object ? A Materialist might argue that material objects existed before conscious subjects ; but, for reasons already mentioned, Hegel held that the stuff of reality was not material substance, but thought. It follows that if the whole universe is like the content of consciousness, subject and object involve one another.

My thoughts are always inside the circle of my consciousness ; hence, as we saw, Leibniz held that monads must be windowless and constitute a universe of solipsists. But Hegel does not talk about *my* thoughts or *your* thoughts ; his Idealism is objective and he talks about *thought*. When he says that a thing (object) is distinct from thought, all he means is that the content of consciousness is extruded or externalized and then viewed as if it were separate from the knower, though it is still knowable. Looked at from one angle, the thing is an object ; looked at from inside, as it were, a thing (as an element of consciousness) is the subject.

How else could the world be the thought of God, and yet God be the thought of individual creatures ? But Hegel calls the one completely real subject the Absolute, and it would be a mistake to regard this as synonymous with a personal Deity. The Absolute is the sum-total of all the categories. It is the whole dialectical series ; it is not something outside, to which the categories apply as defining characteristics. To suppose this is to misunderstand the fundamental principle which Hegel calls *the identity of knowing and being*.

In order to grasp how subject and object can be identical and yet distinct, how various categories involve one another and so give rise to the dialectical series, it is of assistance to know what is meant by logical division and abstraction. Return for a moment to Aristotle, who propounded the useful scheme of classification by genus, species, and differentiæ.

In regard to the use of this scheme for arriving at definitions there are various difficulties which need not concern us now. It is clearly possible to obtain more, and more, and more abstract terms by ignoring individual differences. Thus, if we start with the motley crowd in the street, we can ignore the proper names and divide them into Englishmen and foreigners. Then, by ignoring still more differences, we can arrive at the concept man—for they are all human beings. By continuing the process, we can say they are animals, and still more abstractly that they are lumps of matter.

Now the various sciences halt at one or another of these levels of abstraction—the anthropologist at man, the biologist at animal, and the physicist at matter. It is a convenient and necessary methodological procedure. The metaphysician, however, deals with a still more rarefied abstraction. He is not concerned with matter, still less with individual men; he is concerned with *being*; and according to Hegel, this term is even more abstract than existence. Universals have *being*, but they do not exist.

The universals obtained by the old method are isolated aspects of the totality of things. You can climb *up* the ladder, from individual men to the matter of the physicist; but if you start at the top, you cannot climb down and deduce individual men. It is only as you go up that you find the rungs that you must use. In other words, it would seem that you cannot deduce the more concrete from the less.

This, however, is precisely what Hegel appears to do. He starts from the top of the ladder, with the most abstract concept, *being*; and step by step he deduces more concrete concepts. Being is the genus; not-being is the differentia; becoming is the species. On whether this process is legitimate or not depends the whole stupendous system of the Dialectic.

The traditional method of arriving at a definition may be illustrated by what is called in logical text-books *Arbor Por-*

phyriana. The following diagram may be regarded as a definition of Man.

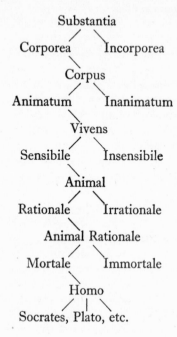

This sort of thing is known as logical division. It is akin to classification. It is supposed to show the essence of a concept. I have deliberately chosen an example of the type of division called dichotomy because it proceeds, as Hegel does, by negating. Thus the genus substance is divided into corporeal and not-corporeal. This procedure would not help Hegel, however. He must negate the term without destroying it, apparently breaking the rule *ex nihilo nihil fit.* Hegel pulls a rabbit out of the hat and indignantly denies that it was ever up his sleeve. Is it a real rabbit, or only the thought of a rabbit ? But, then, he frankly declares that everything is thought. If that be admitted it is not so easy to see where the deception lies. " Is the North pole a real pole ? " asked the schoolmaster. " Could you hang a hat on it ? " To which the schoolboy replied : " It is an imaginary pole and so it would have to be an imaginary hat."

The Dialectic

Hegel will not allow that his categories are imaginary or that abstractions are empty. They are concrete universals, by which is meant that genus does not exclude differentia, but contains it. Being does not exclude not-being in the formal sense that A excludes not-A, according to the principle of contradiction. The genus (being) is indeterminate, and so the passage to species (becoming) is possible only if some determination can be added. This feat is performed by the second term of the triad, which is always a negative. The negation of a concept therefore lies hidden in it ; when it is drawn out we get a determinate third term. The main-spring of the dialectical process is " the portentous power of the negative."

A few examples may make this difficult conception clearer. Being is negated by not-being, and the contradiction is reconciled in becoming. Then becoming collapses, but this does not mean a return to pure indeterminate being. We get, instead, the idea of determinate being, abstract quality, from which we derive limit, then the infinite, then the one and the many, and so on almost in the manner of the House that Jack Built.

The Absolute Idea is equivalent to all reality. It contains the triad : (a) the Idea in itself or Logical idea ; (b) the Idea outside itself, or Nature ; (c) the Idea for itself, or Spirit. These are further subdivided : (a) Being, Essence, Notion ; (b) Mechanics, Physics, Organics ; (c) Subjective Spirit, Objective Spirit, Absolute Spirit. And these, again, contain innumerable sub-categories.

It is impossible to wander through the maze of details. I have done my best to avoid technical terms, but a few must be noted. Hegel's logic employs the triadic form that we have already seen—with few exceptions. The first term is the thesis ; its negation is the antithesis ; and the negation of the negation in the third term is the synthesis. The synthesis shows the unity of opposites ; but it is a new affirmation, and so this in turn is shown to be self-contradictory. The process continues until we find all contradictions reconciled in the Absolute Idea.

Hegel distinguishes between understanding (*Verstand*) and Reason (*Vernunft*). To understanding, opposites appear as mutually exclusive ; but to Reason, difference and identity are not incompatible. " Logical doctrine has three sides : (*a*) the Abstract side, or that of the understanding ; (*b*) the Dialectical, or that of negative reason ; (*c*) the Speculative, or that of positive reason."

" Immediate " is a puzzling term. The thesis is regarded as being characterized by " immediacy " ; and the antithesis by " mediation." What is immediate is simple and self-identical ; what is mediate shows differences, distinctions.

Another term is " moment," virtually a factor. Thus thesis and antithesis are moments of synthesis. The double function of the synthesis to abolish and yet preserve, to unify opposites without destroying their difference, is called sublating, from the German *aufheben*.

Finally the idea of one concept being contained in another, so that it can be deduced from it dialectically, is expressed by saying that it is implicit, or " in itself " (*an sich*). A flower in this sense is implicit in a seed. As Aristotle might have said, the seed contains the flower potentially. Becoming is implicit in being. That is why it can be deduced from it. Every earlier term in the dialectic contains the later terms implicitly. And the later terms contain the earlier ones explicitly, for nothing is lost in the progress from category to category, and there is a steady gain in concreteness until we reach the Absolute Idea, in which all contradictions are resolved and all things are contained.

The Purpose of the Universe

Hegel's Logic ends with the Absolute Idea. Its categories are pure concepts, and the attempt to deduce sensuous concepts has yet to be made. Hegel seems just a little disdainful of mere Nature. He became very angry when a correspondent wrote and asked him if he could deduce the pen with which he was writing.

There is no general agreement among Hegel's followers on this point. But it seems to me to be crucial. If the universe is regarded as a series of thoughts which involve each other, the sensuous concepts of nature can also be deduced—including the pen of Hegel's correspondent, a certain Dr. Krug.

The transition from the categories to Nature, from the inner viewpoint to the outer, is the weakest part of Hegel's scheme. It obliged him to lay down the law about physics, chemistry, astronomy, and biology. After such a grandiose start, such audacious claims, we are entitled to expect a new light to be thrown on science. But Hegel perpetrated such sad nonsense that even the faithful blush.

Dr. W. T. Stace writes : " It is not necessary for the student to enter elaborately into the detailed deductions of the philosophy of nature. It is almost universally admitted, even by the most ardent Hegelians, that this branch of the system, depending as it does upon physical science for its data, is now out-of-date owing to the strides which physical science has made since Hegel's day. Nor will anyone now dispute that, even in his own time, this philosophy of Nature was, as regards the details of its deductions, mostly a failure." (*The Philosophy of Hegel.*)

Hegel was not content to deduce Nature. He applied the dialectic to history, to social institutions, to the development of religion, morals, and art. All religion leads up, by an inexorable dialectical process, to Christianity, which is the absolute religion. (Islam is conveniently omitted from the scheme.) In like manner, the evolution of the State leads up to the Prussian monarchy, a deduction which was very popular with the Government of the day and which provided the Germans with a heady wine in the century of expansion that followed.

The final realization of the Absolute Idea, however, is in

philosophy—and philosophy comes to a stop with the revelation made by Hegel. This is the final, absolute knowledge, the end towards which the rest of Nature, even the stellar galaxies, has moved in slow, inevitable procession. The universe has a purpose. Its purpose is the establishment of Prussian hegemony and the flowering of Hegelian philosophy. That little man, with the furrowed brow and bright blue eyes, mumbling incomprehensibly in a crowded lecture room, represents the supreme self-expression of the Absolute—a claim beside which the most extravagant assertion of Papal Infallibility seems modest indeed.

He enjoyed immense popularity, and he died on November 14th, 1831, a victim of the cholera epidemic—or, as the Greeks might have said, of *hubris*.

Useful References

The Secret of Hegel, by J. H. Stirling; 1865.

The Philosophy of Hegel, by W. T. Stace.

What is Living and What is Dead of the Philosophy of Hegel, by B. Croce; Eng. trs., 1914.

The Logic of Hegel, by W. Wallace.

Studies in Hegelian Dialectic, by J. McTaggart; 1896.

The Phenomenology of Mind, trs. by J. B. Baillie; 1910.

The History of Philosophy, trs. by E. S. Haldane; 1892.

The Philosophy of Fine Art, trs. by F. P. B. Osmaston; 1920.

CHAPTER NINE

The Aftermath of Hegel

THE influence of Hegel was widespread and profound. The fortunes of the metaphysicians were at a low ebb when Hegel came to their rescue. Suddenly it looked as though the glories of speculative philosophy were about to be restored and that the tottering empire had been saved from the scientific barbarian. The dream of the deductive Rationalists seemed about to be realized. " Everything that is real is rational, and everything that is rational is real."

Hegel had surveyed the whole history of philosophy from a fresh point of view. Instead of regarding his predecessors as opponents to be refuted, he searched painstakingly for what seemed of value in their contributions. He believed that every important philosopher had said something that was true, the truest thing that *could* have been said at the time ; the falsity lay in the incompleteness of the vision.

Plato had spoken truly about one aspect of reality, Aristotle about another ; and those who followed—Descartes, Leibniz, Spinoza, and Kant—had also seen truly within the limits of their perspectives. Even the empiricists had made valuable contributions. As Hegel expressed it : " The philosophy latest in time is the result of all preceding philosophies and must therefore include them in itself."

The Realization of the Idea

Consider, for example, the development of ideas as described in the earlier sections of this book. We have seen how the questions asked by one philosopher led to new questions, and so on in an apparently endless series. Heraclitus raised the problem of Change. Parmenides raised the question of Permanence. This gave rise to the problems of Reality and Appearance, the One and the Many, the Universal and the Particular.

If the whole discussion could have taken place between men sitting in the same room it would be evident that every fresh contribution was countered by a denial, which led to a new formulation. Indeed, more than that, every line of thought led to its opposite.

The Materialism of the Ionians led to the Objective Idealism of the Eleatics. The Rationalism of Descartes gave rise to the Empiricism of Locke. Descartes started from an Idealist premise. He claimed that what we were most certain of was a spiritual fact—the reality of the thinking self. Yet Descartes was the father of mechanical Materialism.

Spinoza started out to justify a rational system of knowledge. Unless everything in the universe was interconnected, how could real knowledge be possible ? Yet he fathered a school of thought, culminating in Bradley, which was driven to the conclusion that *because* of this inter-connection genuine knowledge was impossible and science was incurably false.

Again, the sober common-sense of Locke, seeking to anchor beliefs firmly to experience, led straight to the Immaterialism of Berkeley ; and the line of thought opened up by the latter, a vision of the world as a series of volitions in the mind of God, a universe of spirits, led to the denial by Hume of any spiritual reality—a scepticism which extended equally to matter and causation. In the end, however, Empiricism performed yet another somersault, and offered a justification of scientific knowledge ; still more astonishing, the Idealism of Hegel gave rise to Materialism in some of his followers.

Perhaps I should not say " in the end," because there is no finality in these developments. Whatever view we hold of Hegel we certainly cannot believe that the Absolute Idea attained perfect self-realization between 1800 and 1830. But there is some plausibility in Hegel's doctrine that philosophy has developed by discovering the contradictory nature of its theses—that, to express it simply but inaccurately, things turn into their opposites.

Nor is this apparent process confined to philosophy and argument. Something of the sort seems to happen in history. Situations arise that are self-defeating. After the Puritanism of the Commonwealth there was the Restoration. As has long been observed, there is " the swing of the pendulum." Nevertheless, you never *quite* get back to the earlier state. No man crosses the same river twice.

Hegel's explanation was audacious. The Absolute Idea is seen unfolding in history, in philosophy, and in the mind of the individual man. Always it follows the same law of development. It develops like an argument—which is what one would expect if the universe consists of logical categories. A statement is made, or a situation arises ; but the statement, or the situation, is self-contradictory ; at a certain point the contradiction becomes intolerable, and it bursts, giving rise to a new affirmation, a new situation. The process is then repeated.

But, to some extent, Hegel proves too much. For once it is granted that Hegel himself is not the incarnation of the Absolute Idea, Hegel's philosophy must be itself the victim of the Dialectic. It must contain inner contradictions and lead on to its opposite. Oddly enough it does.

Right-wing and Left-wing Hegelianism

There are two very different lines of development possible, and as in fact they led to opposite political trends it is convenient to speak of Right-wing and Left-wing Hegelianism. The Right-wing in Germany were delighted with the news that the rise of Prussia was the manner in which the Absolute realized itself. Most of Hegel's followers in this country also took comfort in the conservative aspect of his philosophy. " Whatever is, is right." So meddlesome people who sought to reform society were blasphemers against the Absolute. " The State is the divine idea as it exists on earth. . . . The State is the march of God through the world."

By assuming that the dialectical series had reached its final

I

term, or by ignoring the Dialectic altogether (like Bradley) Hegelianism could be turned into a mystical justification for preserving the *status quo*. Thus, in *The Secret of Hegel* (1865), J. H. Stirling wrote : " Is it not indeed to Hegel, and especially his philosophy of ethics and politics, that Prussia owes that mighty life and organization she is now rapidly developing ? Is it not indeed the grim Hegel that is the centre of that organization which, maturing counsel in an invisible brain, strikes, lightning-like, with a hand that is weighted from the mass ? But as regards the value of this organization, it will be more palpable to many, should I say, that while in constitutional England, Preference holders and Debenture holders are ruined by the prevailing commercial immorality, the ordinary holders of Stock in Prussian Railways can depend on a safe average of 8·33 per cent. This, surely, is saying something for Hegel at last."

No doubt it is. Left-wing Hegelians, however, drew a different conclusion. For them the secret of Hegel was not the Absolute Idea, but the Dialectic, with its revolutionary implications. It would be wrong, I think, to call these implications " evolutionary." If the Absolute is retained, it is obvious, as Bradley pointed out, that perpetual progress is impossible. The Absolute may realize itself, and so give the appearance of change, but as it is perfect it cannot improve itself. What is even more to the point, the transition from antithesis to synthesis is a leap. It is a sudden transformation. There is nothing about it of " the inevitability of gradualness."

The Left-wing Hegelians felt that the Dialectic justified progress by revolution. They found the Absolute as embarrassing as the Right-wing groups found the Dialectic, and so they left it out. They dismissed the Idealism and substituted Materialism. As Marx expressed it : " in Hegel's writing Dialectics stands on its head ; one must turn it the right way up again."

This may seem somewhat cavalier treatment of a complex philosophical system. Like all systems of deductive rationalism, Hegelianism had a dangerous weakness ; it rested like a pyramid on its point. It was not broad-based, like empirical philosophies, which can endure a very great deal of alteration A mistake in the first step of a deductive system brings the whole edifice tumbling down.

Dialectical Materialism

Marx, however, believed that the metaphysical basis could be destroyed without injury to the essential structure, which he took to be the Dialectic. Instead of Spirit he wrote Matter. This offshoot of Hegelian philosophy is known as Dialectical Materialism. It is of some practical importance to try to understand it because it is usually regarded as the official philosophy of the Soviet Union and of Communist Parties throughout the world.

Dialectical Materialism is the name given to the philosophical scheme first sketched by Marx and Engels, then developed by Lenin and his successors. It is not the outcome of one man's thinking; it denotes a school of philosophy rather than the finished scheme of a single thinker. Moreover, it lays no claim to finality.

Consequently there is no text-book to which one can appeal for an authoritative statement on all the problems under discussion. Marx's views are scattered through writings on economics and sociology. There is, of course, Engels' *Dialectics of Nature*, but a great part of this book is concerned with nineteenth-century science and is correspondingly dated. Lenin's *Materialism and Empirio-Criticism* is a polemic against a number of writers, many of whom have been forgotten, but Maurice Cornforth's *Science versus Idealism* brings it up to date by applying the same method of criticism to Bertrand Russell and the Logical Positivists.

Various books have been published in this country dealing with special aspects. Professor J. B. S. Haldane has shown the application of Marxism to biology, Professor H. Levy to physics and mathematics, Professor G. Thomson and Professor B. Farrington to ancient history, and Christopher Caudwell (among others) to literature and art. The very distinguished group of scientists and writers who have been wholly or partly converted to Marxism is sufficient proof that it is a living philosophy. It is all the more regrettable that no reliable and comprehensive text-book exists for the English reader, and that in so many discussions the same quotations are regurgitated *ad nauseam*.

It is, of course, possible to hold, without being a Dialectical Materialist, that Marx said many wise and important things about economics and sociology. One need not be a Communist to believe that he was substantially right when he argued that Capitalism was essentially unstable. But it was a remarkable achievement to have demonstrated this at a time when it looked to most people as though Capitalism would last for ever.

Again, it showed astonishing insight to perceive that an ideology could be regarded as a function of the social structure. It was a most fruitful hypothesis, and it threw a new light on the re-discovery of the past that gained such pace in the latter half of the nineteenth century. Its importance to the theory of religious origins was missed by the majority of Marx's Rationalist contemporaries.

One can accept a great deal of what Marx had to say about the actual world, however, without accepting the scheme that he took over from Hegel. He elected to express himself in the terminology I have tried to explain in the previous chapter. The shadow of Hegel fell just as heavily on Engels and Lenin.

Indeed, I doubt if the ordinary reader who has never studied Hegel would find their pronouncements intelligible. It is all there—the Union and interpenetration of Opposites, the transition from Quantity into Quality, the negation of Negations, Thesis, Antithesis, Synthesis, and even Moments. But it is there with a difference—the self-realizing Idea has become self-moving Matter.

Dialectical Materialists complain of misrepresentation when they are charged with being metaphysical. They seem to assume that this is equivalent to the charge of Idealism. It is important to remember that practically all other philosophers are classified by them as either " Idealist " or " Mechanist," and, although they repudiate metaphysics as casting a slur on their strictly scientific outlook, they are equally antagonistic to empiricism.

The claim is sometimes made that the Dialectic is not to be regarded as *a priori* truth, but merely as a hypothesis that can be used as an instrument for exploring the world. The empirical demand for a practical test is freely accepted—and no instance has been found, it is said, of the Dialectic being wrong. If, however, every problem is formulated in Hegelian terms, this is not surprising.

The Meaning of Matter

It seems to most people that Dialectical Materialists are just as confident as the seventeenth-century Rationalists that they have found a ground plan of the universe. They hold a form of monistic Materialism; hence their high regard for Spinoza. They certainly show no enthusiasm for the anti-metaphysical philosophers who attacked the whole procedure of deductive Rationalism.

The universe is said to form a single system. That is the first assumption. This system is composed of a single stuff, and the stuff is matter. Whatever exists is matter ; and matter is endowed with the primary quality of self-locomotion. How, then, do other qualities arise ? They arise because this self-movement of matter brings about combinations in such a way that at certain critical points changes of quantity result in changes of quality.

Hegel, it will be recalled, did not begin with matter, or even with substance—or even with quality. He was searching for an explanation. He felt that it was impossible to give a *reason* why things are as they are, if you start with something arbitrary, such as God or matter. For Hegel the dialectical process flows like an argument from the most abstract to the concrete. That was why he felt obliged to hold that material things were thoughts.

The Dialectical Materialist takes the opposite view. Thoughts are material things. The dialectical process is a material process. It is logical ; but logical facts are, in a sense, physical facts. The matter in the brain, which produces arguments and what are called ideas, is fundamentally the same stuff as that of which the earth and the stars are composed. This self-moving matter is the logical subject of every proposition, and it weaves the patterns of biological evolution and human history. All exhibit the fundamental law of the Dialectic.

According to Engels, " Matter moves in an eternal cycle, completing its trajectory in a period so vast that in comparison with it our earthly year is as nothing ; in a cycle in which the period of highest development, namely the period of organic life with its crowning achievement—self-consciousness—is a space just as comparatively minute in the history of life and of self-consciousness ; in a cycle in which every particular form of the existence of matter—be it the sun or the nebula, a particular animal or animal-species, a chemical combination or decomposition—is equally in transition ; in a cycle in which nothing is eternal, except eternally moving matter and the laws of its movement and change. But however often and pitilessly this cycle may be accomplished in time and space, however many countless suns and earths may arise and fall, however long it may be necessary to wait until in some solar system, on some planet, appear conditions suitable for organic life, however many countless beings may fall and rise before, out of their midst, develop animals with a thinking brain that finds an environment that permits them to live, be it even only for a short period, we are, nevertheless, assured that matter in all its changes remains eternally one and the same, that not one of its attributes may perish, and that the same iron necessity which compels the destruction of the highest earthly bloom of matter —the thinking spirit—also necessitates its rebirth at some other place, at some other time." (*Dialectics of Nature.*)

Engels is trespassing on the territory of the physicist. This world may pass away, but matter will remain, and may give rise by " iron necessity " to fresh worlds and new forms of life. How far this conflicts with the prediction of the running-down of the universe which some scientists make I am not competent to judge.

The Emergence of the New

Matter, on this view, although a substance, is not a mere support of qualities. Nor, we are warned, must the " iron necessity " be confused with teleology or purpose. Nevertheless, configurations of self-moving matter can be relied upon to develop dialectically from Capitalism to Communism on this planet, and there may be reason to hope that life will arise elsewhere after the end of our own world.

We must not regard matter as static stuff, but as *moving* substance. " The object is a moving substance," Engels writes. " It is possible to know the different forms and aspects of the substance itself through movement ; only in movement are the properties of a body revealed ; there can be nothing to say of a body that is not found in movement. It follows that out of the forms of movement flow the properties of the moving bodies."

This entails the notion of process. Engels speaks of " the great basic thought that the world is not to be comprehended as a complex of ready-made *things*, but as a complex of *processes*, in which the things apparently stable, no less than their mind-images in our heads, the concepts, go through an uninterrupted change of coming into being and passing away, in which, in spite of all temporary retrogression, a progressive development asserts itself in the end."

So the universe is a complex of material processes at various integrative levels, the laws of which show a direction of movement. Mechanism is rejected, but the Victorian belief in progress is retained. Progress is guaranteed by the iron law of the Dialectic. Lenin writes : " Two fundamental (or is it the two possible ? or is it the two historically observed ?) conceptions of development (evolution) are : development as decrease and increase, as repetition ; and development as a unity of opposites (the division of the one into mutually exclusive opposites and their reciprocal correlation). The first conception is dead, poor, and dry ; the second is vital. It is only this second conception which offers the key to understanding the ' self-movement ' of everything in existence ; it alone offers the key to understanding ' leaps,' to the ' interruption of gradual succession,' to the ' transformation into the opposite, ' to the destruction of the old and the appearance of the new.''

There are several formulations of the three basic laws of Dialectic. These laws are as follows :—

(1) The Unity of Opposites, sometimes called the Identity of Opposites, the Identity of Contradictories, the mutual penetration of Opposites.

(2) The Negation of Negations or the Transformation of Opposites.

(3) The Transition of Quantity to Quality.

According to Hegel, " Identity is the definition only of a simple, immediate, dead being, but contradiction is the root of all movement and vitality, and only in so far as a thing has in itself contradiction does it move, does it possess an impulse and activity. Contradiction is not simply the negation of normality but is the principle of every self-movement, of that which indeed is nothing else than the expression of contradictions.''

The motive-power of the self-movement of matter which results in the emergence of novelty is, therefore, the contradiction to be found within given processes. Engels maintains that contradiction is objectively present in Nature and is " an actual force as well." (*Anti-Duehring.*)

" The existence of two mutually contradictory aspects, their conflict and their flowing together into a new category," wrote Marx, " comprises the essence of the dialectical movement." The opposites do not remain at separate poles ; rather, as Hegel taught, not-being passes back into being and gives rise to becoming. Or as Engels says, ". . . to hold that basis and consequence, cause and action, identity and difference, being and essence, are unalterable opposites, will not bear criticism. Analysis shows the presence of one pole in latent form within the other, that at the determined point one pole goes over into the other and that all logic is developed only from the moving of these two opposites in one another's direction.''

The negation of the thesis is itself negated, yielding the synthesis. According to Lenin : " Dialectical ' moment ' requires an indication of ' unity ' ; i.e., of the connection of the negative with the positive, requires the finding of this positive in the negative. From affirmation to negation—from negation to a ' unity ' with the affirmation ; without this, dialectic becomes a barren negation, a word-play or scepsis."

The Law of Contradiction

The process is illustrated both by Hegel and Engels by the example of a seed. Engels writes : " In dialectic to negate does not mean simply to say ' no,' or to declare a thing to be non-existent or to destroy it at will. . . . I must produce the first negation in such a way that there should be or should become possible a second negation. But how do I attain this ? According to the special nature of each particular case. If I ground up a grain of barley, or crushed an insect, then, though I should have accomplished the first act of negation, I should have made the second impossible. For every category of objects there is thus a special mode of negation peculiar to it, and only from this is development to be obtained."

It is important to note that in this passage Engels admits quite frankly that not *all* movement is dialectical. " I must produce the first negation in such a way that there should be or should become possible a second negation." That the process is *made* to work is one of the commonest criticisms, and has been applied to a further example which Engels gives. " The same is true in mathematics. Let us take any algebraic magnitude whatever, say, a. If we negate it, we have $-a$ (minus a). If we negate this negation, by multiplying $-a$ with $-a$, we have $+a^2$, i.e., the original positive magnitude, but at a higher level, namely, the second power." (*Anti-Duehring.*)

But, as Professor Sidney Hook objects, this works only with the aid of deliberate assistance. For the negation of minus a can be written $-(-a)$, which is not a^2 but a, and so we are back where we started from. With regard to the barley seed, Professor Hook remarks : " Here, as elsewhere, Engels relapses into the Aristotelian doctrine of essential natures—a conception which is incompatible with the dictum he accepts from Hegel, that the nature of a thing is equivalent to the sum total of all of its appearances and is not a structure existing behind, separate from, or in opposition to them. If anything can be ' negated ' undialectically this is just as much a part of its nature, and may be just as important for purposes of scientific inquiry and human welfare, as the fact that it can be ' negated ' dialectically." (*Polemic, No. VI.*)

Can the process be expressed in other than Hegelian terms ? An attempt is made by Professor H. Levy in *A Philosophy for a Modern Man*. He writes : " Consider a given state or situation S, in which there resides a certain quality Q which is undergoing intensification. S has an internal structure or composition, of such a nature that the intensification of Q arouses in it or intensifies in it a structural quality q. The quality q is recognized by the fact that its intensification is inimical to the continued existence of the given state S. Accordingly at a critical stage of q, the state S is transformed by it into a new qualitative state T. The transformation is made manifest by the fact that what was *given* for the state S no longer has relevance. The immediate cause of this intensification of q to its critical value is Q ; the immediate cause of the transformation is q. A change-over brought into being by an internally aroused agency such as q is referred to as a *dialectical change*. . . . The actual quantitative point of q at which dialectical change occurs is referred to by Dialectical Materialists as the point at which ' Quantity passes into Quality ' or more shortly as the *dialectical point*. A statistical isolate involving the co-existence of Q and q prior to the dialectical change is considered as possessing a *contradiction*. The quality q is said to *negate* the state S, and reaches its climax when it is itself transformed in the new situation and plays a new role therein."

Knowledge and Truth

Dialectical Materialism has not developed a detailed Theory of Knowledge. At first sight it may be mistaken for a form of simple Realism. Thus Lenin defines matter as " the objective reality of the external world which exists independently of consciousness and is reflected in consciousness." But it would be an error to suppose that this means that the individual brain passively reflects the outer world like a mirror, in a mechanical way.

The word " reflection " must not be taken too literally. Knowledge is not contemplative, but active and emerges from social practice. Theory and practice, disjoined by the contemplative idealist, must be united. As Lenin says : " At first —impressions, as in a flash, then—something is distinguished, then—ideas of quality are developed (leading to a definition of a thing or phenomenon) and subsequently ideas of quantity. Then study and reflection direct the thought to questions of identity and difference—basis—essence. All these ' moments ' or steps of knowledge are directed from the subject to the object, verify themselves by practice and proceed through this verification to truth."

To obtain truth we must take into account all the aspects of a situation in their mutual relationships. " The aggregate of *all* the aspects of a phenomenon, their actuality, and their mutual dependence—that is the source of truth," says Lenin. But in practice we cannot discover *all* the aspects and relations, so our picture of reality is always incomplete, though it approximates more and more to completeness as knowledge is extended.

" So this dialectical philosophy dissolves all conceptions of final, absolute truth, and of a final, absolute state of humanity corresponding to it. For it nothing is final, absolute, sacred. It reveals the transitory character of everything and in everything ; nothing can endure before it except the uninterrupted process of becoming and of passing away, of endless ascendancy from the lower to the higher." (Engels, *Ludwig Feuerbach.*)

Note " the endless ascendancy from *lower to higher*." The powerful psychological appeal of these logical abstractions is due to the promise the dialectic seems to give that there must be an end to human frustration and exploitation. In Marx's famous words : " Capitalist monpoly becomes a fetter upon the

method of production which has flourished with it and under it.
The centralization of the means of production and the socializa-
tion of labour reach a point where they prove incompatible with
their capitalist husk.   This bursts asunder.   The expropriators
are expropriated."

This is not, however, a fatalistic doctrine.   It would be useless to sit down and wait for the transformation to take place.
Individual men must work and fight to bring the change about ;
but, regarded on the group level (and laws are statistical, or
about groups, not about individuals), final success may be confidently predicted.   " With the inexorability of a law of nature,
capitalist production begets its own negation.   It is the
negation of a negation.   This second negation does not re-
establish private property, but it does re-establish individual
property upon the basis of the acquisitions of the capitalist
era ; i.e., on co-operation and the common ownership of land
and of the means of production (which the labour itself produces)."

Science and Ideology

It is impossible to deal with all the aspects of Dialectical
Materialism, but some mention must be made of a difficulty
that many people feel.   A theory of knowledge which makes
experience depend on social practice and which regards the
concepts used as social products has to justify its own claim to
be valid knowledge.   In other words, if Marxism is " true "—
indeed if any scientific theory is to be regarded as even approxi-
mately " true "—it cannot be *merely* the reflection of a transitory state of affairs.

We owe to Marx and Engels a view of ideology that is widely
accepted to-day and would be defended by many who are not
" Marxists " if science were excluded from ideology.   Indeed,
when some Catholic apologists argue that the causes of the
Reformation were more economic than theological, they echo
Marx.   When Egyptologists, like Breasted, argue that ancient
monotheism was a reflection of ancient imperialism, they confirm one part of the Marxian thesis.

It would be tedious to multiply instances. We are familiar nowadays with the psychological term " rationalization," an early example of which was the fox's declaration that the grapes he could not reach were sour. An ideology can be regarded as a collective rationalization. Although Engels sometimes writes as though this sort of wishful thinking is to be contrasted with the reality-thinking of science, the modern Dialectical Materialist inserts science within the superstructure.

According to Engels : " Ideology is a process which, of course, is carried on with the consciousness of so-called thinkers, but with a false consciousness. The real driving force which moves it remains unconscious, otherwise it would not be an ideological process. It imaginatively creates for itself false or apparent driving forces." From this it would appear that since Marxism claims to be a science it must be exempt from the self-deception that it exposes. And it would seem that the theories of such exact sciences as physics and chemistry must also be exempt.

Here, however, we come to the parting of the ways between the tradition of experimental philosophy and the tradition of speculative philosophy. Those who believe that ideology is a mass-rationalization of motives, but regard this proposition as an hypothesis verified by history, are following the traditional scientific method. They feel that they must not cast doubts on the conceptual instrument they use to test the hypothesis. For them the problem does not belong to philosophy but to empirical science.

But the modern Dialectical Materialist objects to this procedure. He is scornful of those who accept some parts of Marxism and reject others. He regards even science itself as an ideology, and for several reasons. In the first place, if the concepts used by science are social products, they must be modified by their social environment. In a Capitalist society they will be contaminated by the false thinking that Capitalism generates. In a Socialist society they will be less contaminated, and in a Communist society there will be an even purer approximation to truth. Thus *bourgeois* science cannot compete with

Marxian science, for the Dialectic opens the only door to an undistorted knowledge.

Again, there is the purely metaphysical argument that, despite its contradictions, all reality is one and indivisible. The universe forms one system. All propositions can be reduced to one form—the attribution of a property to a subject. The universal subject is Matter, and it realizes itself in the manner revealed by the Dialectic, pretty much as Hegel believed the Absolute Idea to realize itself—but so conceived it leads far beyond the Prussian Monarchy to Communism. The real is the rational, and so there is a gradual approximation towards rationality which means that even Dialectical Materialism itself progresses and becomes more completely true.

The attitude of modern Dialectical Materialists towards science is lucidly stated by Christopher Caudwell in *The Crisis in Physics*. He affirms unambiguously that scientific theories are part of an ideology. " The categories of science, or ' things seen,' always reflect in a class society the particular conditions of functioning of the working class. . . . The categories of mind—of philosophy, art, and mystical religion— always reflect in a class society the particular conditions of functioning of the ruling class as felt by them."

Man " interpenetrates " actively with nature, and as a scientist he gives information *to* society. His language is therefore socially conditioned. " When the *bourgeois* considers matter as the object of cognition he is unable to conceive of it except under the categories of mechanism." These are said to be atomism, strict causality, absolute time and space.

And so, according to Caudwell, " the philosophy of physics is the philosophy of all *bourgeois* in relation to matter. It is mechanical Materialism. The philosophy of all *bourgeois* philosophers in relation to matter is the same ; but for various historical reasons *bourgeois* philosophers ceased to be interested in matter and developed another part of *bourgeois* philosophy, that concerned with mind or subjective reality."

We learn that even the monadology of Leibniz " is simply dogmatic materialism under another name " and that " the

' theological ' God of the seventeenth-century thinkers is really matter." Again: "The mentalism and tendency towards anti-scientific scholasticism of modern physicists is not a result of their researches, for it denies the method by which they were achieved. . . . The crisis in physics is a part of the final crisis in *bourgeois* economy, which gives rise to revolution and the creation of a new economy."

USEFUL REFERENCES

Appearance and Reality, by F. H. Bradley; 1893.
Towards an Understanding of Karl Marx, by S. Hook; 1933.
From Hegel to Marx, by S. Hook; 1938.
Aspects of Dialectical Materialism, by Hyman Levy, and others.
Dialectics, by T. A. Jackson; 1936.
Marxist Philosophy and the Sciences, by J. B. S. Haldane; 1938.
The Crisis in Physics, by Christopher Caudwell.
Illusion and Reality, by Christopher Caudwell.
Science versus Idealism, by Maurice Cornforth; 1946.
Soviet Philosophy, by John Somerville; 1946.
A Handbook of Marxism, Ed. by Emile Burns; 1936.
Ludwig Feuerbach, by F. Engels, Eng. ed.; 1934.
Anti Duehring, by F. Engels, Eng. ed.; 1935.
Dialectics of Nature, by F. Engels, Eng. ed., with Intro. by J. B. S. Haldane; 1941.
Empirio-Criticism, by Lenin, Eng. ed.; 1928.
A Textbook of Marxist Philosophy, prepared by the Leningrad Institute of Philosophy under the direction of M. Shirokov; 1937.

CHAPTER TEN

The Universe of Science

THE tremendous uprush of philosophical activity that culminated in Kant and Hegel made very little impression on the experimental philosopher. He had been told that he was merely dealing with appearances, that matter did not exist, that to search for causes was vain, that such concepts as absolute space and time, forces, and infinitesimals were self-contradictory and absurd. Arguments that he certainly could not refute were advanced to prove that what he was doing was impossible and that the whole venture was doomed to failure. He went on doing the impossible with almost uninterrupted success.

It was not, of course, the sort of success at which speculative philosophers had aimed. Theoretically it was inferior and partial. It did not reveal the ground-plan of the universe, but it showed that bits of the universe at least were orderly, and the sort of laws discovered enabled predictions to be made.

Instead of explaining knowledge, science added to knowledge ; and instead of analysing change, science effected real and even spectacular changes. This was an intolerable situation, a logical scandal that the critics could not ignore, and so philosophy had somehow to account for it. Dialectical Materialism was but one of a number of attempts by philosophy to come to terms with science.

To-day we can see rather more plainly that the business of the philosopher is not to tell the scientist what to do, but to make clear what he is doing. The concepts that the scientist uses and the way he uses them form an intellectual instrument more powerful—judged by results—than anything man has ever devised, and the philosopher can be well employed in sharpening and refining this tool in a creative partnership with those who use it.

The question that arises, therefore, is, What is this instrument? What are the rules, and can the existing method be improved on? The Hegelian Dialectic also claimed to be a new *method* of discovering truth. What other methods are there?

In the nineteenth century the Dialectic was used by Marx to advance economics and social science; but it was not employed by anyone in the physical or biological sciences. The instrument used by the majority of scientists was something very different, and it led in an almost unbroken line from Galileo, Kepler, and Newton to Dalton, Faraday, Darwin, and thence to Freud, Einstein, Bohr, and the contemporary invasion of science into every department of knowledge.

The Worship of Reason

The first philosophers to recognize that science must be taken very seriously indeed were the Encyclopedists. They derived much of their inspiration from England, but they drew conclusions from the writings of Locke and Newton that would have shocked both those Anglican churchmen.

They were, of course, very largely concerned with social implications. They were kindling a fire that was to bring the feudal fabric of French society crashing in red ruin. For the Encylopedists the great instrument for solving problems was Reason—though the actual solution, as far as social problems were concerned, was achieved (as previously in England) by force.

Matthew Arnold complained: " The mania for giving an immediate political application to these fine ideas of the reason was fatal. Ideas cannot be too much prized in and for themselves, cannot be too much lived with ; but to transfer them abruptly into the world of politics and practice, violently to revolutionize the world at their bidding—that is quite another thing."

To practice what you preach is always, no doubt—" quite another thing." However, we are not concerned with social

K

philosophy.   In the more abstract fields it can hardly be denied that the men of the Enlightenment were second-rate.   They were mostly mechanical Materialists and they combined this with Atheism or Deism, always with lucidity and sometimes—in the case of Rousseau and Voltaire—with literary genius.

Voltaire (1694–1778) struck the anti-metaphysical note, which was to culminate in Comte's Positivism, by declaring that metaphysics had not advanced since the time of the Druids. "If God did not exist it would be necessary to invent him," he also said—though we must not forget the rest of the sentence, "but all Nature cries out to us that he exists."

Condillac (1750–1780) developed Locke's Sensationalism. All thought can be reduced to sensation, on his view, and it is still possible to read his presentation of empiricism with profit. La Mettrie (1709–1751) also held that all ideas come from the senses.   In *Man a Machine* he developed an uncompromising Materialism.   He said that a State composed of Atheists would be the happiest of all States, for Materialism freed man from a sense of guilt and responsibility, and the fear of future suffering.

In 1770 d'Holbach brought out his famous *System of Nature*, which expanded the same theme.   Matter and motion are eternal and Nature is a self-moving whole, an endless chain of causes and effects.   Man is purely physical and thought is a function of the brain.   Man is the passive instrument of necessity, a cog in the eternally-moving, cosmic machine. When he dies he can be likened to a clock broken into a thousand pieces.   "O Nature, sovereign of all beings, and ye her daughters, Virtue, Reason, and Truth, be forever our only divinities!" he exclaimed, rhapsodically.

Church and State united to stamp out these dangerous doctrines.   The works of Voltaire were burned.   People found in possession of blasphemous literature were branded and sent to the galleys.   One victim of the purge of 1765 was condemned to have his hand cut off, his tongue torn out, his head cut off and his body burned.   We cannot, therefore, be surprised that a note of passion entered the forbidden devotion to the new goddess of Reason.

Reason and Hypothesis

But what is meant by Reason? As a mere antithesis to Faith the concept may serve in the rough and tumble of practical affairs, but obviously a much more precisely defined method is needed by the scientist if he is to make any progress in adding to our knowledge. The scientific results, out of which the Encyclopedists so enthusiastically constructed a philosophy, were not obtained *merely* by being rational. Aristotle was rational, but his philosophy was used as a brake on the development of science. Spinoza was rational, but in what sense can he be said to have contributed to positive knowledge?

The French Materialists tried to run before they could walk. Nobody in the eighteenth century had any right to lay down the law about the inmost nature of the entire universe, or about the human mind. We have only to think of the investigations that still lay ahead to realize how superficial any " System of Nature " must have been.

The point is worth emphasizing because there are still people who believe that the task of philosophy is to weave scientific knowledge into a pattern, patch up the holes with guesses and present the result as a finished picture of reality. To some, the mechanical Materialism of La Mettrie and d'Holbach still appears as a real alternative to a religious cosmogony. At least this sort of Materialism can be easily understood.

The metaphysicians sought certainty—but unhappily they failed to convince anyone that they had found it. The scientists, on the other hand, must not seek that *sort* of knowledge. To say in advance of investigation that everything that exists is matter and obeys mechanical laws is not the sort of statement that a scientist (loyal to his principles) wishes to make. He must not adopt a " take it or leave it " attitude. What he can say, of course, is that *if* the cosmos is a material machine *then* certain consequences will follow. But he will add—Let us put the question to a *test*.

This is a very different way of approaching a problem. In the first place certain facts are selected. The scientist does not deal with every fact. He makes a selection. From the outset he deals only with an aspect of the totality of facts.

He selects moving objects or animate objects or human societies, according to where his interest lies. Then he sets up an hypothesis as a guide to the experiments he proposes to carry out. He observes in order to establish a correlation between things he sees. He invents postulates—new abstract terms—that may or may not be found valuable. He does not regard a single unfavourable observation as necessarily a sign that the hypothesis is untenable. He allows for experimental error.

If the final result is the verification of the hypothesis, what he has supposed might be the case has turned out to be indeed the case. The two different weights dropped from the tower of Pisa land at the same time. The observed movements of the planets are found to be in accordance with the prediction. But if there is a discrepancy the scientist concludes that either the hypothesis is wrong or there is an undetected factor responsible. He may assume, in order to make the hypothesis work, that an unobserved planet exists.

Obviously this is a very simplified account of the procedure. For, once an organized system of verified hypotheses is set up, they are themselves treated as facts, and deductions are made from them. Broadly speaking, this is what experimental philosophy amounts to.

A problem is selected ; a hypothesis is set up ; the hypothesis is developed deductively, and repeated observations are made to test it. The upshot is that a selection of facts is shown to be connected with other facts in a manner that no one would have noticed from cursory inspection. New knowledge, therefore, results. At the conclusion of the experiments it can be said that we may confidently expect to find the property X wherever we find the property Y.

Such knowledge, of course, is not *certain*, in the metaphysical sense. There is always a risk of a more delicate instrument being devised which will show that some previous observations were inaccurate. When that happens a new hypothesis may have to be set up and the process gone through all over again.

Nor is the procedure itself completely free from assumptions. In order to make a beginning it is necessary to assume that the facts under observation belong to a system which is intelligible. Assumptions may have to be made regarding causation and induction. It is not, however, necessary that the facts in the universe should be interconnected in the manner in which Spinoza and Hegel believed them to be. Scientific laws can be framed without assuming that the universe forms a perfectly coherent system in which every fact is dependent on every other fact; all that is necessary is that it should be a deterministic system—one in which every constituent is determined by *some* other constituents.

A great deal of the confusion about the method of science has been caused by the reluctance to admit : (1) that assumptions cannot be altogether dispensed with ; (2) that the knowledge obtained falls short of certitude ; (3) that hypothesis is an important element in the method pursued.

Newton's Four Rules

" *Hypotheses non fingo*," said Newton. " I make no hypotheses." But in the sense in which I have used the word it seems evident that he did not dispense with hypotheses. So much misunderstanding has arisen out of Newton's account of scientific procedure that it is worth while to quote his own words in the *Principia* : " But hitherto I have not been able to discover the cause of those properties of gravity from phenomena, and I frame no hypotheses ; for whatever is not deduced from the phenomena is to be called an hypothesis ; and hypotheses, whether metaphysical or physical, whether of occult qualities or mechanical, have no place in experimental philosophy. In this philosophy particular propositions are inferred from the phenomena, and afterwards rendered general by induction. Thus it was that the impenetrability, the mobility, and the impulsive force of bodies, and the laws of motion and gravitation, were discovered. And to us it is enough that gravity does really exist, and act according to laws which we have explained, and abundantly serves to account for all the motions of the celestial bodies, and of our sea."

That he is affirming the empirical nature of science is at least a possible interpretation. He detested the associations of the word " hypothesis " and protested strongly that an hypothesis was never a demonstration. He believed—as Mill did—that truths could be discovered by the use of induction, and this raises a highly controversial issue. But at least Newton had a very clear idea of what he meant by " reason " as an instrument of discovery.

He laid down the following rules of scientific reasoning. For him they constituted the new intellectual tool of experimental, as opposed to speculative, philosophy.

" *Rule I.* We are to admit no more causes of natural things than such as are both true and sufficient to explain their appearances. To this purpose the philosophers say that Nature does nothing in vain, and more is in vain when less will serve ; for Nature is pleased with simplicity, and affects not the pomp of superfluous causes.

" *Rule II.* Therefore to the same natural effects we must as far as possible assign the same causes.

" *Rule III.* The qualities of bodies, which admit neither intension nor remission of degrees, and which are bound to belong to all bodies within the reach of our experiments, are to be esteemed the universal qualities of all bodies whatsoever.

" *Rule IV.* In experimental philosophy we are to look upon propositions collected by general induction from phenomena as very nearly true, notwithstanding any contrary hypothesis that may be imagined, till such time as other phenomena occur by which they may either be made more accurate or liable to exception."

How admirably lucid all this seems in contrast to the misty profundities of Hegel—and how much more fruitful it proved to be ! Newton, it is true, set himself a more limited problem, but it is hardly an exaggeration to say that the whole of scientific achievement in the ensuing centuries was built on the foundations he so carefully laid. For the scientist—as for Locke—reason and experience were the supreme arbiters.

Can Induction be Justified?

The progress of science and the failure of metaphysics naturally gave rise to a demand for a still more precise definition of method. It became apparent that the experimentalists were working on profitable lines, but why they should obtain such good results was something of a puzzle. It was extremely difficult to find a theoretical justification for the procedure they followed so successfully. The practical man may feel that all that matters is the result, but philosophers take a long view and they hinted darkly that some day the logical sins being committed would be found out in practice.

The philosophers were right in this respect. In its early days science worked with a set of very dubious philosophical concepts. It clung as far as possible to the common-sense view of the world. As Russell has put it : " The development of science out of common sense has not been by way of a radically new start at any moment, but rather by way of successive approximations. That is to say, where some difficulty has arisen which current common sense could not solve, a modification has been made at some point, while the rest of the common-sense view of the world has been retained. Subsequently, using this modification, another modification has been introduced elsewhere, and so on. Thus science has been an historical growth, and has assumed at each moment a more or less vague background of theory derived from common sense." (*Analysis of Matter*, p. 133.)

What was wrong with the common-sense view which scientific procedure presupposed ? What, it may be asked, is wrong with Newton's rules of reasoning ? The main trouble can be indicated very briefly—the use of inductive logic and the assumption of a universal law of cause and effect. The two things really go together. It is the problem of arguing from past to future generalizations.

Newton's law of gravitation is an example of induction. From a limited number of observations—and obviously everything in the cosmos cannot be observed—a generalization is made about *all* moving bodies. The force of gravity is said to be the *cause* of the way they move. A cause (as we have seen) was rejected by Hegel as a satisfactory explanation. He rejected it because he believed that an explanation should proceed deductively, not inductively.

This may be further illustrated by the proofs of the existence of God at which we have already glanced. The ontological proof deduces the existence of God from the concept of a perfect Being; the argument is that the idea of perfection contains existence. But the proof that because the world is orderly there must be a source of order, or because there is design there must be a Designer, can proceed inductively, like the search for a First Cause. Hence many philosophers who have believed in the law of universal causation have been Deists.

In traditional logic, however, the argument by induction errs by taking an illicit leap from the particular to the general. The abstract form of the argument is as follows : " All observed A's are B's. Therefore all A's (including those unobserved) are B's." This will not do. All observed crows are black ; but we cannot rule out the possibility of a white crow, unless we say that being a crow implies being black, in which case we are merely making a definition.

Is there any way of defending the inductive procedure ? I think it would be widely acknowledged to-day that there is no way—if we require that it should lead to universal and certain knowledge. One contemporary solution is to re-state the argument in terms of probability. " All observed A's are B's, therefore it is *probable* that all A's are B's."

This is good enough for the scientist ; it is more or less what Locke had said, and why he took a restrained view of the prospects of scientific knowledge. He did not realize—nor did any of the pioneers of the empirical method—that probability, rightly understood, is a very real kind of knowledge. But it is a different kind of knowledge from what the metaphysicians so desperately and so vainly sought. And there are many un-solved problems about the meaning of probability.

The Philosophy of Mill

An attempt was made by John Stuart Mill to show that empiricism could compete with metaphysics in giving certitude. Mill was a brilliant thinker, and, although many of his con-clusions cannot be accepted to-day, he made an important contribution to the clarification of scientific methodology. I propose to deal only with this aspect of his work.

Following Comte, he rejected metaphysics outright. Comte supplied the name " Positivism " to the movement which had really begun with the English empiricists. Comte himself was a somewhat preposterous figure, and the extraordinary esteem in which he was held by so many nineteenth-century worthies in this country can be accounted for only by their unworldly simplicity and Victorian earnestness. I shall, however, use the term Positivism as a synonym for scientific empiricism.

Mill not merely repudiated deductive rationalism, but also the Kantian compromise. He held that there were no *a priori* truths. All knowledge was obtained from experience. We know that twice two are four because we have observed that this is the case. The laws of logic and the law of universal causation are likewise derived from experience. As for the material world, Mill coined the famous phrase that " Matter is a permanent possibility of sensation."

There is " no principle, which, antecedently to any verifica-tion by experience, we are compelled by the constitution of our thinking faculty to assume as true." So much for innate ideas and Kant's categories. How, then, do we discover true principles ?

By denying the right to use any principles not derived from experience Mill set himself a hard problem ; and by refusing to admit the necessity to make any assumptions, he rendered the task of demonstrating the basis of science well-nigh im-possible. There is no doubt that he was wrong in believing that all general truths are arrived at inductively from experience.

Russell has since shown that in the proposition " $2 + 2 = 4$ " we are merely expressing the meaning of four, as we express the meaning of a yard by saying it equals three feet. But Mill was right in perceiving that science rests upon induction. He goes on to argue, however, that induction is derived from causation, and that causation is vouched for by experience.

He defines induction as " the process by which we conclude that what is true of certain individuals of a class is true, in similar circumstances at all times."

He admits that induction is not primary, that it involves an assumption. " We must first observe that there is a principle implicit in the very statement of what induction is ; an assumption with regard to the course of Nature and the order of the universe ; namely, that there are such things in nature as parallel cases ; that what happens once will, under a sufficient degree of similarity of circumstances, happen again, and not only again, but as often as the same circumstances recur."

But, he insists, uniformities *are* actually found in Nature. There are uniformities of co-existence (" All crows are black ") and uniformities of succession. The latter give us the idea of causation, and induction depends on this idea. " The Law of Causation, the recognition of which is the main pillar of in-ductive science, is but the familiar truth that invariability of succession is found by observation to obtain between every fact in Nature and some other fact that has preceded it." He amplifies this : " Invariable sequence is not synonymous with causation, unless the sequence, besides being invariable, is unconditional. There are sequences as uniform in past experience as any others whatever, which we do not regard as cases of causation, but as conjunctions in some sort accidental. Such, to an accurate thinker, is that of day and night."

Causes can be observed in operation. To set up a law of cause and effect is merely to generalize from what we see. The chief task of the scientist, according to Mill, is to search for causes. When a cause has been found the occurrence in-vestigated has been " explained." Generalizing from a set of observations—the result of a number of experiments—is the sort of inductive reasoning that enables us to state a law which is basically of the form that certain effects will always follow from certain causes.

The final set of observations, exemplifying this law, is arrived at by experiment, for which Mill lays down four canons. These amount to saying that we must vary the factors, one at a time, so that by a process of elimination we arrive at the required result. That the discovered cause should *always* operate does not seem to him a great difficulty. He scarcely seems to grasp Hume's real problem. For Hume did not deny that observations suggest causal uniformities. Hume asked what the connection was between one fact and another which could *compel* invariable sequence ? Mill seems satisfied to say that we can see that this is so—and because it is so now, it must be so always and everywhere.

Consequently he held that induction is " the operation of discovering and proving general principles." The results of induction are scientific propositions characterized by universality and certainty.

He is not always either clear or consistent. But there is no doubt that he helped to formulate the creed of many working scientists. They would agree that, if science is to continue, it must make use of inductive reasoning. If induction is possible, there must be a law of cause and effect. If there is a law of cause and effect, it will be evident from observation. We do, in fact, observe cause and effect ; therefore induction is legitimate ; therefore science is possible.

The Development of Positivism

Mill's philosophy has an air of glorified common sense. It seems a mere quibble to doubt that there are necessary uniformities in Nature, or that the search for causes is legitimate, or that generalizations from a large number of observed facts are permissible. But when Mill triumphantly produces Newton's theory of gravitation as an example of induction providing a law which is both universal and certain, the " quibble " is seen to have some basis. Since Mill's day

Newton has been partly supplanted by Einstein, and it would be rash to suppose that Einstein has said the last word.

The truth seems to be that the empirical scientist cannot entirely dispense with assumptions. Induction does not yield metaphysical certainty. Still less can it be maintained that the truths of mathematics are learned from experience.

An attempt, later in the century, to evade the difficulty by regarding scientific laws as mere descriptions of phenomena— abbreviations of what is observed—was prompted by Kirch- hoff's definition of Mechanics as " the science of motion ; we define as its objects the complete description in the simplest possible manner of such motions as occur in Nature."

This is a highly sophisticated variety of Positivism, developed by Avenarius, Mach, Ostwald, and Karl Pearson. It is the " empirio-criticism " castigated by Lenin. It is a vigorous reminder that ultimately the data of the scientists is the world of sensible appearance, and that unobservable entities— atoms, for example—must be capable of being re-translated into elements of ordinary experience. Science, particularly physics, was becoming so abstract that there was a danger of its abstrac- tions being hypostasized as " things-in-themselves," of cutting adrift " the world of reason " from " the world of common sense."

We shall return to this later. Mill in his way, Mach and Pearson in their way, sought to keep the feet of the scientist on empirical ground. We can still maintain that, whatever else may be said of science, its main concern is with experience, its duty (as Berkeley stressed) is to think concretely, its safeguard is experiment, and its enemy metaphysics.

To avoid metaphysics, to remain true to its empirical origin, science has had to sacrifice certitude to probability, for it is only in terms of probability that inductive reasoning can be rendered valid. And probability, according to J. M. Keynes, requires that two assumptions should be made about the nature of the universe. We must assume (1) " that the objects in the field, over which our generalizations extend, do not have an infinite number of independent qualities ; that, in other words, their characteristics, however numerous, cohere together in groups of invariable connexion, which are finite in number." This is the Principle of Limited Independent Variety. In addition, we must assume (2) that " the system of the material universe must consist . . . of bodies which we may term (without any implication as to their size being conveyed thereby) *legal atoms*, such that each of them exercises its own separate, independent, and invariable effect, a change of total state being compounded of a number of separate changes each of which is solely due to a separate portion of the preceding state." Keynes calls this the Principle of Atomic Uniformity.

In other words, we must suppose, though we cannot prove, that what we investigate belongs to a system of a certain sort. The rich variety of objects presented in experience must be reducible to manageable proportions. The actual number of units may be infinite, but their qualities must not be infinite, or we can never hope to make reliable laws. In practice this sort of reduction is found to be quite possible, and the more science develops, the more probable such initial assumptions seem to be.

Hume's question has not been satisfactorily answered. But it is much clearer to-day than ever before what science is doing and what *kind* of knowledge it offers us. There are differences of opinion about the meaning of such terms as " law " and " probability," but the controversies to which they have given rise have greatly enriched our understanding.

What has vanished is the picture of the universe as a vast piece of clockwork, operating under an iron law of cause and effect, composed of material atoms to whose changing positions in absolute space and time every statement can be reduced. Nor is the universe now regarded as a mysterious, unknowable " something " lying beyond the range of our understanding. It is very close to us indeed ; the physical " universe " is largely a system of relations of our own devising, an interpretation of experiences which cross the threshold of consciousness un-invited. As Einstein says : " The object of all science, whether natural science or psychology, is to co-ordinate our experiences and to bring them into a logical system." How far this involves complete subjectivism is one of the most difficult problems of contemporary philosophy.

USEFUL REFERENCES

A Century for Freedom, by Kenneth Urwin.
An Introduction to Modern Logic, by L. S. Stebbing; 1933.
The Philosophy of Auguste Comte, by Levy-Bruhl; 1903.
Positive Philosophy, by Auguste Comte, 5 vols.; 1830-42.
A System of Logic, by John Stuart Mill; 1843.
Auguste Comte and Positivism, by John Stuart Mill; 1865.
A History of European Thought in the Nineteenth Century, by J. T.
    Merz; 1896-1912.
Contributions to the Analysis of Sensations, by Ernst Mach; 1897.
Scientific Thought, by C. D. Broad; 1923.

CHAPTER ELEVEN

The Problem of Change

THE Hegelian Dialectic was an attempt to solve the problem of change. It was encumbered by the doctrine of the Absolute, which is timeless. Why the Absolute should generate the time-process—or the illusion of it—is not made clear. Dialectical Materialists dropped the Absolute, but they retained the notion of substance. To the question, " *What* changes ? " they replied, matter changes. There is nothing outside which makes it change. The motive-force is internal. It must not be sought in isolated particles, but in the grouping of these particles. Contradictions develop within these groupings, and at a certain point a new quality appears.

On the whole, a simpler view was held by the majority of scientists. Consider, for example, the changes that can happen to water. Suppose it starts as ice ; heat is applied and it melts ; more heat is applied and it becomes steam. We say that ice changes into water, and water changes into steam.

Now water can be analysed into oxygen and hydrogen. These can be lumped together as *matter*. The change of matter from one form (liquid) to another form (gas) is held to be due to the movement of material particles. (" Heat is a mode of motion.") These particles move about, and to describe this we require the dimensions of space. The process of passing from solid to liquid to gas may be expressed by saying that the water *was* solid, *is* liquid, and *will be* gas, if the heat is maintained. In other words, the change takes time, and time involves the ideas of past, present, and future.

And so the doctrine gained ground that change could be accounted for by the concepts of matter, motion, space, and time. The whole universe consisted of material particles in

motion, and their positions in space and time could (in theory)
be predicted. A human being also consisted of material
particles, and in theory you could predict his behaviour. You
could not merely predict eclipses, but cast the world's horo-
scope.

Qualities need not be considered. They are merely the way
mind reacts during this mechanical process. The colours we
see, the sounds we hear, the scents we smell, are mental aspects
of changing matter. The sole reality in nature is the material
particle. To this attractively simple and once plausible theory
Whitehead protests : " the entity, bared of all characteristics
except those of space and time, has acquired physical status
as the ultimate texture of Nature ; so that the course of
Nature is conceived as being merely the fortunes of matter
through space and time."

And this recalls Berkeley's objection that " matter," so far
from being the concrete object given in experience, is merely a
logical abstraction. " Thus Nature gets the credit which should
in truth be reserved for ourselves," Whitehead continues,
ironically : " the rose for its scent ; the nightingale for his
song ; and the sun for his radiance. The poets are entirely
mistaken. They should address their lyrics to themselves, and
should turn them into odes of self-congratulation on the excel-
lency of the human mind. Nature is a dull affair, soundless,
scentless, colourless ; merely the hurrying of material, end-
lessly, meaninglessly." (*Science and the Modern World.*)

Such indeed was the view of the French Materialists. To
make it more palatable, it was sometimes attached to Deism.
In addition to the machine, there was God. Herbert Spencer
(1820–1903) compromised with Agnosticism. He held that
the sphere of religion was the unknowable ; the sphere of
science was the knowable. And all we can know are the laws
governing the hurrying to and fro of material particles in the
abysses of space.

The philosopher's task, according to Spencer, is to co-ordinate scientific knowledge and discover (by abstraction) the
general principle from which all movement can be deduced :

" to interpret the phenomena of life, mind and society in terms of matter, motion and force."

Darwin published the *Origin of Species* in 1859, and Spencer's *First Principles* came out in 1862. Evolution seemed to fit beautifully into Spencer's scheme. He argued that all phenomena are subject to " an integration of matter and concomitant dissipation of motion ; during which the matter passes from an indefinite, incoherent homogeneity to a definite, coherent heterogeneity ; and during which the retained motion undergoes a parallel transformation."

Thus the master-principle is " the persistence of force " ; and Spencer seems to have thought that this meant the persistence of progress, for the evolving forms pass from lower to higher. But he also envisaged " alternate eras of evolution and dissolution."

The Revolt Against Mechanism

Spencer has had little influence on contemporary philosophy. The immense superstructure that he erected rested on mechanistic foundations. They were undermined in his own lifetime as much by scientists as by philosophers. He never seriously touched the central problem of change : how can something genuinely *new* appear ? The Dialectical Materialists saw more clearly what the problem entailed. At rock-bottom it was—as Parmenides himself perceived—a problem of logic. It was a problem that may be forever insoluble if rendered in terms of substance and accidents.

Obviously, for this purpose it is not very important what you *call* the stuff of which the world is composed. If it is an independent substance, whether you call it *materia prima*, or matter, or energy, or hydrogen, or electricity, or even mind, is beside the point. Such a single substance, which merely moves, cannot undergo changes, other than those of position, that yield totally new qualities. Either you must juggle in some way with the concepts of quality and quantity, in Hegelian fashion, or transfer the problem to the observing mind.

Bergson tried a wholly different approach. He did not start

L

with matter and try to explain change ; he started with change and tried to explain matter. He concluded that matter is a mistake. The intellect gives a false picture. In order to analyse what is actually in continuous flux we petrify it in thought—we treat time as space. We cannot, of course, help doing this when we think scientifically. Science relies on the intellect and freezes or " spatializes " the process it examines. For example, you cannot dissect a living brain ; for you kill it in the very act of cutting it up. And you " kill," or rather falsely arrest and spatialize, the ceaseless becoming.

When we ask " *What* changes ? " we usually think of a number of states rapidly succeeding each other, like a cinematograph, giving the illusion of continuous movement. We think of motion, perhaps, as made up of " immobilities" or static pictures. Hence, says Bergson, we mistake the fictions of analysis for reality, which is pure becoming. We are thus unable to solve the problem of Zeno's arrow, which moves, although at any instant it is stationary.

It is curious to see Zeno's conundrum cropping up again on the threshold of the twentieth century, in the guise of a cinematograph. Russell has answered it as follows : " A cinematograph in which there are an infinite number of pictures, and in which there is never a *next* picture because an infinite number come between any two, will perfectly represent continuous motion. Wherein, then, lies the force of Zeno's argument ? " (*History of Western Philosophy*.)

Bergson was rash enough to dogmatize about mathematics, and Russell has dealt with him perhaps too severely. It follows from Bergson's argument that science has taken the wrong road. Knowledge of reality is not given by the spatializing, falsifying intellect, but by intuition, which is a higher development, in man, of animal instinct. In this way we learn that the past still exists, that the process of becoming adds to it like the rings of a tree, and that this process is not the mechanical evolution of Spencer, but is *creative* evolution. It is no dreary passage of matter from homogeneity to heterogeneity, but the expression of the *élan vital*, the creative Life-Force (which Bernard Shaw substituted for God).

The reaction against mechanism led Bergson to a decidedly mystical outlook as hostile to science, in its different way, as Bradley's *Appearance and Reality* (1893). Evolution made no great impression on Bradley. He held firmly to what William James called "the block universe." For Bradley, scientific knowledge is partial knowledge. To know anything truly you must know everything. There is not much point in talking of evolution or progress if all things that exist—the physical universe, the entire animal kingdom and the human race—are but adjectives of the Supreme Noun.

Bradley is a curious example of a philosopher whose great influence on his contemporaries stimulated them on the whole to form quite other conclusions than his own. He left many admirers, but no disciples. The tide in the nineties was running too strongly with the scientific philosophers. Nevertheless another attempt was soon to be made to express the fact of evolutionary change in non-mechanistic terms.

Emergent Evolution

Lloyd Morgan and Samuel Alexander have enriched our vocabulary by adding the term "emergent." Evolution, on their view, is not mechanical. If it is construed in terms of matter and force you should be able to predict (theoretically) the whole course of it. Consequently nothing really *new* would ever appear. But the essence of the changing world in which we live is the emergence of genuine novelty. To dismiss this novelty as mind-dependent and secondary is an evasion.

Mechanism fails, therefore, to account for so-called secondary qualities. It may be convenient, but it is no solution, to attribute them to the mind. You still have to explain mind and its contents. You may know all about the molecules that make up ammonia, and all about the molecules that make up the mucous membrane, but from such data alone you could not predict the precise *smell* of ammonia. Again, nothing that is known about oxygen and hydrogen separately would lead us to predict that in combination they would yield all the qualities that we know water to possess.

This situation is not due (as the mechanist might protest) to ignorance. It is due to the fact that the properties of a whole cannot be deduced *merely* from the constituents into which a whole is analysed. The quality of a tune is something more than the mere sum of its parts. This " something more " is the emergence of the genuinely *new*. This sort of quality is called an *emergent quality*.

In *Space, Time, and Deity*, Alexander advances a cosmo-logical theory that is materialistic without being mechanistic. In the beginning was Space-Time, the most abstract entity conceivable. Its only empirical quality at this stage is motion. It is somewhat like the self-moving matter of the Dialectical Materialist, but it is not yet complex enough to be physical matter. In the course of its self-development Space-Time acquires the emergent quality of materiality ; then it acquires the emergent quality of Life, then of Mind, and next . . . the new quality, towards which the world is straining, the shadow of things to come which already touches us, is Deity. This the theory of the unborn God who did not make the world but who emerges from it. The physical world is (or rather, will be) God's body.

It may be wondered how, if the whole point about emergent qualities is that they are unpredictable, we can nevertheless predict that the next quality will be Deity. Of more import-ance is the logical issue that emergent evolution raises. Berg-son's objection to analysis was confused by mysticism, but this is very different. It is a materialistic challenge to much of scientific method.

To what extent must we falsify the changing world when we analyse it ? Our answer to this question will place us into one or other of the two great camps into which philosophy was dividing at the beginning of this century. The cleavage is more fundamental than the traditional distinctions between Materialism and Idealism. What the world is made of and the place of mind in it are questions which must be answered *after* we have decided on our logical procedure. The issue is not between material atomism and some spiritual theory of reality, but between logical atomism and what may be called organic theories.

Spinoza, Hegel, and Bradley illustrate the organic point of view. So, in not quite such a thorough-going fashion, do the theories of Dialectical Materialism, Creative Evolution, and Emergent Evolution. Locke regarded a general term (a whole) as a convenient way of naming a bundle of particulars. He was therefore an atomist. Such a way of looking at " wholes " is condemned by the organic philosophers. They complain that it leads us to regard the world as a machine ; and the atomists retort that if we abandon the cinematographic view we are driven towards mysticism, for intellectual analysis then becomes impossible and we fall back on intuition and bad mathematics.

The complex currents of thought which reformulated the struggle between rationalists and empiricists as a choice between organism and atomism, under the pressure of rapidly changing scientific conceptions, found their expression in two philosophers who started as collaborators and then sharply deviated. Whitehead and Russell were joint authors of *Principia Mathematica* (1910–1912), but, although they accepted revolutionary changes in our ideas of logic, they applied the new logic very differently. Russell became a logical atomist and Whitehead elaborated a system which he called " the philosophy of organism."

The Philosophy of Organism

The time has gone when philosophers could construct systems in rivalry to science. Nowadays the most interesting contributions to philosophy are made by scientists and mathematicians. The modern philosopher has not merely to know something about evolution ; he has to take into account the consequences of the far more difficult theories of Relativity and Quanta. He may even be required to express an opinion on pure mathematics. Almost impossible demands are made upon him.

Alfred North Whitehead (1861–1948) possessed these quali-fications. He was a brilliant mathematician and a classical scholar. He knew exactly what the new physics was about and he had studied traditional philosophy long and deeply. He was not the sort of man to be bamboozled or to rush in with some hastily constructed, home-made theory of his own. Indeed, he did not publish his first purely philosophical book, *Science and the Modern World*, until he was 63. His chief work, *Process and Reality*, was brought out at the age of 68, and it was evidently the fruit of lifelong meditation and profound learning. No one could doubt that a major philosopher had appeared in our midst.

I do not think it is an exaggeration to say that to-day we must choose between the *type* of philosophy represented by White-head and the *type* represented by Russell. Whitehead has advanced a defence of metaphysics and a criticism of Positivism that are unlikely to be improved upon. He represents a com-promise between metaphysics and empiricism. One of his most solid achievements has been to devise a technique for expressing the relationships of such metaphysical conceptions as points and instants in terms of sense-data, thus realizing the empirical ideal. This technique is called " the method of extensive abstraction."

To give a concise summary of Whitehead's philosophy is impossible. The subject-matter is unusually difficult, but although Whitehead can write prose of great beauty and find a phrase that breaks as a sudden illumination in the darkest places, he can also write with an almost Hegelian obscurity. Moreover, he has invented a special terminology of his own, and to make things harder he applies such words as " feeling," " satisfaction," " aim," and " society," to inanimate Nature in a way which is consistent enough with his principles, but very confusing to those labouring to understand him. He enjoins us to seek simplicity yet mistrust it ; but it must be confessed that in his writings the mistrust is more evident than the search.

For Whitehead, speculative philosophy (metaphysics) is an

endeavour to provide a set of ideas in terms of which everything we experience can be interpreted. ". . . I mean that everything of which we are conscious, as enjoyed, perceived, willed, or thought, shall have the character of a particular instance in the general scheme." The purely scientific scheme, he argues, leaves some elements out. A mechanical view of the universe is a result of treating the abstractions of physical science as though they were concrete elements of experience. This is " the fallacy of misplaced concreteness."

Unlike the traditional metaphysician, he does not claim that his own scheme is final. On the contrary, it is a tentative and imperfect attempt to devise a language with which we can correlate all our experiences.

But experience must not be conceived subjectively. Whitehead is a Realist. He will not allow that even secondary qualities are contributed by mind. We experience a world of colours, scents and sounds. In the *Concept of Nature* he writes : " Nature is what we observe through the senses." He repudiates " Nature bifurcated into causal Nature and apparent Nature." He will not accept the Kantian compromise " that our perceptual experience does tell us of a common objective world, but that things perceived are merely the outcome for us of this world and are not in themselves elements in the common world itself." (*Science and the Modern World.*)

The world we experience at any given moment is seen in " the mode of presentational immediacy." Subjectivist philosophers, imagining that all knowledge comes in this manner, naturally regard the external world, succession in time, and causation, as inferences. They try to justify these inferences. They fail because they disregard the other mode of experience which Whitehead calls " causal efficacy." Our body takes notice of " causal efficacy " whatever our brain may do. We see a flying bomb falling and we take cover—we don't stop to reason about it. Lower animals act purely on " causal efficacy." For man, knowledge results from the interplay between presentational immediacy and causal efficacy. This mixed mode of perception is called " symbolic reference." It involves interpretation.

There can be no mistakes about what is immediately presented. What is experienced is a fact. But you can make mistakes when you try to interpret the fact. Hume's subjectivism and the Kantian " bifurcation of Nature " arise from the false supposition that causal efficacy has to be inferred from presentational immediacy. The truth, according to Whitehead, is the exact contrary. " The notion of causation arose because mankind lives amid experiences in the mode of causal efficacy."

Generally speaking, says Whitehead, we shall find that adjectival words express information derived from the mode of immediacy, while the substantives convey our dim percepts in the mode of causal efficacy. We see a patch of grey ; but when we interpret it as a stone, we feel, with Locke, that there must be some substance supporting the quality, and that " power is a great part of our complex ideas of substances."

A Universe of Events

I have already traced the uneasy history of the concept of " substance." Many philosophers have been dissatisfied with it, but every attempt to do without it led to wildly improbable conclusions. Whitehead shows us how to dispense with it and yet retain an external world with causes and effects. He is able to do this because physics has shown the notion of a substratum to be superfluous. The Theory of Relativity substitutes events for material particles ; and Whitehead (although he has a different theory of Time from Einstein's) takes events as the bricks of his universe.

This is a difficult idea. It is best not to try to imagine it. " The notion of empty space, the mere vehicle of spatial interconnections, has been eliminated from recent science. The whole universe is a field of force, or in other words a field of incessant activity " (*Modes of Thought*). The units of this field are occurrences, not solid particles *to which* something occurs. There is no mysterious underlying substance called

" matter," corresponding to that presupposed by the grammatical subject of everyday sentences. There are just happenings —and the relations between these happenings.

The life of the earth is a happening ; so is the life of an individual, say, Julius Cæsar ; so is a moment in Julius Cæsar's life ; " and so is the most trivial puff of existence in far-off empty space." Consequently real things are not bits of matter, but activities or " actual occasions." A string of occasions is what we ordinarily call a physical object. A stone, for example, is a strand of history—a route of occasions set in the infinitely complex pattern of routes which make up the universe.

Events in a field of activity spread their influence far and wide, like a stone thrown into a pool and causing ripples. There is no difference, from this point of view, whether you throw a stone on a piece of hard ground or into a pool ; there are ripples in both cases. Every event is related to every other event ; they reflect each other, like the monads of Leibniz, and they modify each other. They enter into the composition of each other. A thing is what it is and where it is because of all the other things in the field of activity. A thing is wherever its influence is felt, and so " in a certain sense, everything is everywhere at all times."

This rather dark saying is merely a forceful way of denying what Whitehead calls " simple location," or " the simple-minded theory that an object is at one place at any definite time and is in no sense anywhere else." The truth is that " each object is in some sense ingredient throughout Nature." To ascribe simple location to an entity is to assume that " it can be said to be *here*, in space, or *there* in time, or here in space-time, in a perfectly definite sense, which does not require for its explanation any reference to other regions of space-time." (*Science and The Modern World.*)

" The volumes of space," he continues, " have no independent existence. They are only entities within a totality ; you cannot extract them from their environment." And elsewhere : " any factor by virtue of its status as a limitation within the totality, necessarily refers to factors within the totality other than itself." Indeed, " nothing in Nature could be what it is except as an ingredient in Nature as it is." So every bit of reality is inextricably entangled by internal relations with the rest.

How, then, is knowledge possible ? It is possible because actual happenings achieve an individuality. " The physical field is luckily atomic," Whitehead writes. Otherwise " every statement would require a detailed expression of all the facts in nature." This breakdown of the essentiality of relatedness is too complex a question to be discussed now. Unlike the classical advocates of the " block universe," Whitehead starts with concrete facts, with the events we experience in all their diversity and individuality, and then searches for the general characters of which they are instances ; he does not deduce, in Hegelian style, the concrete from the abstract. There are stubborn, individual facts, coming into existence and passing out of it ; but they are nevertheless involved during their passage in a web of relatedness.

The Mystery of Time

If there were no coherence, no order of Nature, science would be impossible. As an historical fact, Whitehead points out, science developed because of the Greek conviction that Fate imposed such an order. The spatio-temporal order of Newtonian physics, however, must be replaced by a relational theory of space and time. Events are " the relata of the fundamental, homogeneous relation of extension " from which space and time are both derived. They are constructed from the overlapping of durations.

The measurable time of physics must not be confused with " the passage of Nature," or duration. The process of becoming, whereby one event is succeeded by another, which it modifies, shows " the continuous inheritance of a certain identity of character transmitted throughout an historical route of events."

The influence of Bergson may be detected in Whitehead's distinction between " duration " and the measurable time of physics. And, perhaps, the influence of Alexander may be seen in the following passage from *Religion in the Making* : " The universe is passing with a slowness, inconceivable in our measures of time, to new creative conditions, amid which the physical world as we at present know it, will be represented by a ripple barely to be distinguished from non-entity. The present type of order in the world has arisen from an unimaginable past and it will find its grave in an unimaginable future. There remains the inexhaustible realm of abstract forms, and creativity, with its shifting character ever determined afresh by its own creatures, and God, upon whose wisdom all forms of order depend."

This is typical of those imaginative flights with which Whitehead rewards the reader, somewhat exhausted by the aridity of long, abstract speculation. But the intellectual excitement of such passages must not be allowed to conceal their essential difficulty. On the face of it, Whitehead is suggesting a cosmic evolution not unlike Alexander's theory of the gradual self-enrichment of Space-Time by the emergence of new empirical qualities.

But surely, we are tempted to protest, this is inconsistent with the relative theory of time. If the total assemblage of events, which is the universe at any moment, is advancing towards greater complexity, achieving a more intense individuality, surely the whole bundle of local times adds up to something very like absolute time. One answer—and I am not at all sure that it is the right one—would be that Whitehead's objection to absolute time is only an objection to Newtonian time, with its assumption of bits of matter. In other words a distinction is made between cosmic, psychological, and physical time.

Cosmic time is the passage of durations, and a duration is a cross-section of Nature limited by simultaneity. Durations are what we experience, mathematical time is what we construct. We do not *experience* the " instants " required for a mathematical series. " The passage of Nature has no narrow ledge of definite instantaneous present within which to operate. Its operative presence must be sought throughout the whole, in the remotest past as well as in the narrowest breadth of any present duration. Perhaps also in the unrealised future. Perhaps also in the future which might be, as well as the actual future which will be."

Time measurements are obtained from the fundamental relation of durations of extending over each other. We can construct in this way an indefinite number of time-systems, any one of which can be used in a description of physical events. What Whitehead believes he has accomplished is to dethrone " the trinity of materialism : (1) the temporal series of extensionless instants ; (2) the aggregate of material entities ; (3) space which is the outcome of relations of matter."

The Return to Plato

The mere philosopher would be well advised to leave this sort of thing to the mathematical physicist, and it is at least certain that in any such dispute Whitehead is well able to hold his own. But a good deal more is involved in his picturesque account of the evolution of the universe than a theory of time. The Platonic character of the language will be noticed. And for this Whitehead makes no apology.

He claims that certain Platonic concepts need very little adaptation to provide the general ideas for which he is searching in order to interpret all that we experience. The whole of it, be it noted—" all the choir of heaven and the furniture of earth." Hence the religious colouring.

The concepts he takes from Plato are, the Ideas (Forms), the Physical Elements, the Psyche, the Eros, the Harmony, the Mathematical Relations, the Receptacle. He says, " These notions are as important for us now as they were then at the dawn of the modern world, when civilizations of the old type were dying." Again : " I have directed attention to Plato's doctrine of the Receptacle because, at the present moment, physical science is nearer to it than at any other period since Plato's death. The space-time of modern mathematical physics, conceived in abstraction from the particular mathematical formulæ which applies to the happenings in it, is almost exactly Plato's Receptacle." (*Adventures of Ideas.*)

It seems to amount to something like this. Instead of bits of matter, the universe is made up of happenings. They are " actual occasions " of experience. You and I perceive them ; that in itself constitutes an event. They perceive us. What we perceive is, to us, an object, in itself a subject.

Perception does not necessarily entail consciousness. It will be recalled that Leibniz used the word in this somewhat confusing fashion. For Whitehead, every actual entity, be it an electron or a philosopher, has a mental and a physical pole. The mental pole of an electron, however, is negligible—except as an illustration of the fact that there are no clear-cut distinctions between dead and living matter. Consciousness and life depend, not so much on the microscopic actual entity as on the macroscopic organization of entities.

We do not encounter isolated actual entities. They all belong to some background, which modifies them. It is therefore possible that an electron in the social organization of the human brain is in some ways different from an electron in a crystal—just as a citizen of Russia is different from a citizen of the United States or from Robinson Crusoe. There are societies of electrons within a molecule, societies of molecules within a blood corpuscle, societies of blood corpuscles within a human body, societies of bodies, planets and so on. The whole universe is a society of societies of societies, etc.

The fact that laws are social accounts for the statistical laws of science. They express relationships between groups. The fact that the universe is evolving, and that laws express the characteristics of levels of organization, implies that no laws can be immutable. As the cosmos slowly passes from one " epoch " to another, some laws will cease to apply, others will have to be discovered. Thus laws are not to be thought of as imposed from above, by a transcendental law-giver ; nor are they mere descriptions of observed behaviour. They are "immanent"—expressing the real connectedness, and so the nature, of happenings.

But to return to the microscopic point of view, the string of actual occasions which constitute, let us say, a molecule. Whitehead usually restricts the word " event " to the whole string, and refers to the atomic unit as the actual occasion. Each occasion can be analysed into universals (which White-head calls Eternal Objects) and into what is particular and unique for the occasion.   Its uniqueness is to grasp other components of the universe into a unity.   When that unity is achieved, the occasion attains " satisfaction."   It is self-completed.   It perishes.   But not without transmitting something of itself to the next occasion—thus the future conforms to the past.

Consequently there are " routes of occasions."   A molecule is just such a route—like a cinematograph reel.   The difference between the pictures on the reel, the succession of occasions, constitutes the change or movement of the molecule.   There is no material substance which changes and yet remains the same— that ancient paradox of philosophy.   There is only a succession of occasions, which perish as soon as they complete themselves and are " objectified " in other occasions by entering into their composition—as an object enters a subject.

The Demiurge

We can see, I think, how this applies to our conscious experience.   The originality of Whitehead's view is that the same sort of language is used of what we ordinarily call material objects.   He calls this process of completion, or satisfaction, which is the " aim " of all things, " concrescence."   It is a manifestation of the creative advance of the universe—of what he calls " creativity."   We require an ordering principle to account for the fact that out of an infinite variety of possible worlds, the actual type of order of *this* world arises.   The principle of concretion is God.

Whitehead's conception of God is as unusual as nearly everything else in his philosophy, and it is a little surprising that it should have been given such a welcome in theological circles. God, says Whitehead, is neither omnipotent nor ominiscient.

He is " not the author of the play." He is " not to be treated as an exception to all metaphysical principles, invoked to save their collapse. He is their chief exemplification." Nevertheless " He is the principle of concretion—the principle whereby there is initiated a definite outcome from a situation otherwise riddled with ambiguity." This is the primordial nature of God, " the unlimited conceptual realization of the absolute wealth of potentiality."

Thus viewed He is " deficiently actual." But " the consequent nature of God is conscious ; and it is the realization of the actual world in the unity of his nature, and through the transformation of his wisdom." On the other hand, " He does not create the world, He saves it : or more accurately, He is the poet of the world, with tender patience leading it by his vision of truth, beauty, and goodness." (*Process and Reality*.)

Whitehead adds a list of antitheses which does little to illuminate the obscurity of these pronouncements. " It is as true to say that God is permanent and the World fluent, as to say that the World is permanent and God fluent. . . . It is as true to say that God transcends the World, as that the World transcends God. It is as true to say that God creates the World, as that the World creates God."

For my part, I must frankly confess that I am unable to understand this language. But there are times when Whitehead seems to give us a glimpse of a profound wisdom which makes all the effort to follow his difficult reasoning of slight account. Thus, he speaks of " the final end " of creation and the problem of evil as follows : " This end is existence in the perfect unity of adjustment as means, and in the perfect multiplicity of the attainment of individual types of self-existence. The function of being a means is not disjoined from the function of being an end. The sense of worth beyond itself is immediately enjoyed as an overpowering element in the individual self-attainment. It is in this way that the immediacy of sorrow and pain is transformed into an element of triumph." (*Process and Reality*.)

Whitehead has made out the best case that can be presented

at the present time for a compromise with metaphysics. But to his occasional appeals to intuition and his initial assumption that the universe forms a necessary, coherent system, the empiricist will doubtless turn a deaf ear. The detailed information supplied about the primordial and consequent natures of God must elicit the pertinent question : " *How* do you know all this ? How *can* you know it ? "

Whitehead begins very persuasively by saying that he is merely trying to frame the general ideas in terms of which we can interpret what we experience. But it must be admitted that in the ardour of the quest he moves a very long way from the data of experience.

Useful References

First Principles, by Herbert Spencer ; 1862.
Time and Freewill, by Henri Bergson ; 1888.
Matter and Memory, by Henri Bergson ; 1896.
Creative Evolution, by Henri Bergson ; 1907.
Space, Time, and Deity, by S. Alexander ; 1920.
Whitehead's Philosophy of Organism, by Dorothy Emmett ; 1932.
The Concept of Nature, by A. N. Whitehead ; 1920.
Science and the Modern World, by A. N. Whitehead ; 1926.
Religion in the Making, by A. N. Whitehead ; 1927.
Process and Reality, by A. N. Whitehead ; 1929.
Adventures of Ideas, by A. N. Whitehead ; 1933.
The Revolt Against Dualism, by A. O. Lovejoy ; 1930.

CHAPTER TWELVE

The New Logic

THERE are at least two ways of looking at a metaphysical system. It can be regarded as a bold, imaginative picture of a possible state of affairs—" a likely story," as Plato said. We can take flight with the philosopher and try to capture a god-like view *sub specie aeternitatis*. Alternatively, we can, so to speak, X-ray the picture. We can analyse it and try to discover why it has its specific pattern.

This must not be confused with analysing the philosopher. You may conclude that he painted a gloomy picture because he suffered from dyspepsia. You may decide that he is an Idealist because he is a psychological introvert, or because he wants to escape from human society, or because he hates his wife. This sort of analysis may have its uses, but it is not logical analysis.

Logical analysis is concerned with the form in which a philosophy is stated. It is therefore concerned with statements, sentences, propositions. " Traditional elementary logic, taught in youth, is an almost fatal barrier to clear thinking in later years, unless much time is spent in acquiring a new technique," writes Bertrand Russell. Before examining Russell's philosophy it is worth while trying to see what he means, because he so often inveighs against " traditional logic," and I think many readers must be puzzled. Surely, some may think, logic deals with the laws of thought, and these are beyond argument.

Logic deals with more than the *laws* of thought. It deals with *forms* of expression and the rules which enable us to substitute one symbol for another. Some words refer to these symbols, others refer to the rules of manipulation, still others to the facts which sentences express. There can be no argument about primitive facts. They are just *there*, and we must take them or leave them. But there can be a lot of argument about the interpretation of these facts.

What is a fact? If I see a grey patch, that is a fact—it is beyond argument. If I say that the grey patch is a lump of lead I express myself in the *form* of a proposition. To emphasize the difference I call the phrase by which I draw attention to a particular grey patch *demonstrative*, and the phrase which ascribes characteristics *descriptive*.

A description itself need not predicate a property of an individual subject, as the older logicians thought. Whatever else Russell has done he has cleared up the muddle that arises from the doctrine that every proposition has the same form—a subject and a predicate. We will consider this in more detail presently, and meanwhile let us glance briefly at a few examples.

" The husband of Xantippe is mortal " tells us that Socrates is mortal, because we know that the description fits. But the description does not *stand* for an individual in the direct manner of a name, and so it is not really of the subject-predicate form. It really conceals the assertion we have to make that an individual *exists*. When we assert that, we can apply a description to him. Obviously there might be no such person. A great deal of ink has been wasted on describing the appearance of non-existent individuals and supposing that whatever could be talked about, or thought of, must exist.

Confusion has also been caused by general propositions such as " All men are mortal." These, also, are not of the subject-predicate form. " All men " does not denote an individual subject. If it did, a class would be a real entity. We should have to speculate on the substantiality of a class if we treated " all men " in the same way as the individual name, " Socrates." It stands for a collection of individuals ; and it is the case that every one of these individuals is mortal if the generalization is true.

At the base of all knowledge are the individual facts of which we are aware. We know them, as Whitehead says, in the mode of presentational immediacy. But knowledge would remain slight if it were restricted to direct awareness. I am not acquainted with the Pope ; my knowledge of him is descriptive. I do not need to *see* the Pope, however, in order to know the characteristics of being a bishop, and I do not need to have visited Rome in order to know some characteristics of the city of Rome.   And so I can make up a proposition in which the word " Pope " stands for the Bishop of Rome, and I can assert (which may or may not be true) that this description applies to an actually existing man.

As Russell puts it : " I shall say an object is ' known by description ' when we know that it is ' *the* so and so,' i.e., when we know that there is one object and no more having a certain property ; and it will generally be implied that we do not have knowledge of the same object by acquaintance."

The New Technique

Logic does not reveal new facts.   Hegel thought it did ; and so did the learned professors of Padua at whom Galileo laughed so heartily.   A proper appreciation of logic enables us to sort out facts and it clarifies what we mean by knowledge.   Thus a confused view of what we are doing when we classify and connect facts may lead to a vast metaphysical superstructure which rests on a false conception of logic.   That is what Russell means by saying that Aristotelian logic was responsible for bad metaphysics.

Locke, for example, gave a description of a lump of lead— it had a certain colour, shape, and ductility.   Under the influence of tradition he supposed that it was necessary to postulate a material substratum, a mysterious " I know not what " to be the support of those qualities.

When we use the subject-predicate form of sentence (" Lead is grey "), we are all apt to think that there must be something permanent, something which persists through all changes, to which such qualities as greyness can be attached.   Thus the Catholic Church teaches that, in transubstantiation, the colour and shape of the consecrated wafer remain, but the substance is changed—the process is in reverse.

The view that there is no underlying substance cannot be

easily expressed in everyday speech or in the logical forms which take our usual syntax for granted. That is partly why the Einstein theory is so hard to describe in ordinary language. Instead of talking about material particles (substances) it talks about events. And Whitehead has shown, with wonderful ingenuity, how we can regard a material object as a string of events.

Russell agrees with him, in the main, though there are important differences about the implications. Russell will have nothing to do with Whitehead's mysticism. Also, he disagrees with Whitehead's theory that the " aspects " of a thing—which make it "ingredient" throughout the universe—really constitute one entity. In short, Russell sets his face against the organic view, which regards every event as being necessarily related to every other event. He remains a stubborn atomist.

We have no reason, he says, for believing that everything is related to everything else. We must proceed piecemeal. With the aid of certain postulates we can frame laws that seem to apply to the limited region of the universe which we can observe. But we have no right to say, in advance, that everything is subject to law. We must tackle one problem at a time. Some philosophical problems, formerly regarded as insoluble, can now be solved by means of the new logical technique.

He holds that Zeno's problem has been solved. Objective Idealism of the Platonic and Hegelian sort collapses when taken out of its old, logical framework. Such problems as whether universals exist, whether the existence of God and the soul can be proved, whether infinitesimals, mathematical points, instants, and numbers exist, can also be solved by this method. It can be shown that, apart from the set of individuals and the defining property which determines them as a class, there is not another individual which is *the* class.

Before dealing with Russell's general conclusion let us look a little more closely at what he calls " the powerful logical technique of modern analytical empiricism." He writes : " It is thus able, in regard to certain problems, to achieve definite answers, which have the quality of science rather than of philosophy. It has the advantage, as compared with the philosophies of the system-builders, of being able to tackle its problems one at a time, instead of having to invent at one stroke a block theory of the whole universe. Its methods, in this respect, resemble those of science. I have no doubt that, in so far as philosophical knowledge is possible, it is by such methods that it must be sought ; I have also no doubt that, by these methods, many ancient problems are completely soluble." (*History of Western Philosophy*.)

He claims that much worthless philosophizing about the infinite has been exposed by Cantor's definition of an infinite collection as one which has parts containing as many terms as the whole collection contains ; that Kant's theory that arithmetical propositions are " synthetic," and Mill's that they are empirical, are both refuted by the *Principia Mathematica* (in which Whitehead collaborated) ; and that Bergson's theories of time and becoming and number are vitiated by a false conception of continuity, and ignorance of Frege's definition of number (made in 1884).

Russell differs to some extent from Whitehead's theory of how points and instants can be obtained from empirical facts, but all this is in the spirit of the new " analytical empiricism." We need not concern ourselves deeply with this highly technical controversy, but it is as well to see what it is about. In brief, mathematical points and instants are not found in Nature. We always find a point with some magnitude, an instant with some duration. So it has long been a puzzle to the empiricist how such conceptions could apply to the real world.

If mathematics forms a world of its own, well and good ; but there is applied mathematics, as well as pure mathematics, and " points " and " instants " are used in calculations that enable bridges and aeroplanes to be constructed. Whitehead solves this by the Principle of Extensive Abstraction, which Professor C. D. Broad has described as " the prolegomena to every future philosophy of Nature." The solution is curious in that points are endowed with structure.

Picture a nest of boxes, each containing a smaller box. This forms an enclosure series which converges to a limit. But a point is not defined, as might be supposed, as the limit; a point is the whole set of volumes. Briefly a point is a series of volumes that would commonly be said to converge to a point; and at first sight this might seem to justify Jowett's criticism of Logic in general—that it is neither a science nor an art, but a dodge.

I mention this because it seems a good example of the kind of special problems that are being solved by modern philosophers, as opposed to the construction of systems. The above is primarily a mathematical problem, but it has philosophical implications. Whitehead and Russell have tried to show that mathematics develops from logic; and it is scarcely possible to-day to say where logic ends and philosophy begins.

The Theory of Descriptions

One of Russell's most important contributions to logical theory is the discovery of propositional functions. It is not much use complaining about the traditional logic if a new instrument cannot be put in its place. A propositional function is claimed to be just such an instrument.

A propositional function differs from a proposition rather as a blank cheque differs from a completed cheque. "Socrates is human" is a proposition; "x is human" is a propositional function. We cannot say that "x is human" is either true or false; that is how it resembles a blank cheque waiting to be filled in by some word that stands for a fact, unless the cheque is to be dishonoured. Metaphysicians are apt to overdraw their account at the bank.

Now take the statement "Man exists." We may be easily misled by the form of this statement to suppose that over and above Jones and Smith and Brown there exists the class to which they belong, the universal Man. But from Russell's point of view the above proposition is not about "Man" or about "existence," but about a description, "human," which is applied to individuals.

"Man exists" must mean, if it is to be intelligible, that the property of being human is a description that can be applied to at least one existent. It is a poor way of saying that an object exists which has the property of being human. To say "The Pope likes pineapples" is to say that being the Pope, and liking pineapples, can be treated as a joint assertion which is sometimes true. In other words, if *x* has any property, *x* must exist. Or in another way, existence should be asserted only of descriptions.

Russell takes the statement "Scott was the author of *Waverley*." The statement, rightly analysed, means: "One and only one man wrote *Waverley*, and that man was Scott." Or more formally, "There is an entity *c* such that the statement '*x* wrote *Waverley*' is true if *x* is *c*, and false otherwise; moreover *c* is Scott."

To say "Scott exists" is really bad syntax. What we assert is that there is an entity, *c*, which satisfies the propositional function "*x* wrote *Waverley*." As Kant had long ago pointed out, existence is not a predicate. Russell is therefore carrying out most rigorously the line of criticism which Kant applied to the classical proofs of God's existence.

Finally, the old puzzle about whether "round squares" and "golden mountains" were endowed with subsistence by being discussed disappears. "The golden mountain does not exist" means: "There is no entity *c* such that '*x* is golden and mountainous' is true when *x* is *c*, but not otherwise."

So many of our beliefs involve asserting the existence of something that it is essential to see what we mean by making such an assertion. To assert existence is to assert that a certain description or property belongs to something. There is, however, no such property as "being real" or "being thought of."

The Causal Chain

I have spent some time on these points, which at first sight appear to be splitting hairs, because they illustrate how logical analysis goes to work. Much more is involved than re-stating obvious truths in a roundabout fashion. The theory has since been advanced, for example, that scientific laws may be considered as propositional functions and that the problem of induction can be solved by regarding it as the process of formulating singular propositions from propositional functions and verifying them. I will deal with this later.

We can form a pretty shrewd idea, however, of where such logical analysis is going to lead. It leads us, in the first place, back to Hume, with his faulty psychology left out. It leads us to his distinction between " matters of fact " and " relations between ideas."

Matters of fact can be expressed by elementary propositions. Some of these take the traditional subject-predicate form, " Socrates is mortal," or " S is P." Others take the relational form, " Cæsar loves Brutus," symbolized as " a R b " or " R(x,y)." A propositional function is usually symbolized $f(x)$.

Now it is generally held that a proposition must be either true or false. We can deny S is P by writing " It is not true that S is P."

This can be expressed symbolically by treating the form " not-P " as a function of the elementary proposition from which it is constructed—a *truth-function*. For not-P is false when P is true, and true when P is false.

Symbols standing for " not, and, either or, not both, implies," are called logical constants. By manipulating them it can be shown how easy it is to be deceived into thinking we are saying something new, whereas we are saying the same thing in different ways. In other words, the distinction between matters of fact and ideas, or mere symbols, is shown by these technical devices, and the so-called laws of logic turn out to be tautologies, according to Wittgenstein.

Generalizations, such as " All men are mortal," can be reduced to elementary propositions, and their truth depends on the truth of those elementary propositions—on whether or no the instances enumerated are factual. Russell adheres to the correspondence theory of truth. In the last analysis Hume's matters of fact, the impressions from unknown causes, the patch of grey we see, are practically what Russell means by perceptions. They are sense-data. One aim of analysis is to discover whether concepts can be shown to be logical functions of sense-data.

Let us start, then, with individual percepts. From percepts we can construct complicated, enduring objects. The objects of everyday experience—chairs, tables, etc.—are logical constructions. This may seem surprising, but Russell takes the example of a wall-paper. It goes on fading, changing. It is not possible, in the strict sense, to have knowledge of it by acquaintance. Consequently it does not stand for particular constituents of a proposition in the way that a demonstrative symbol (such as " This ") stands for its referent. The word " wall-paper " is said to be an " incomplete symbol "—that is to say, a symbol with no meaning in isolation from a context.

" When we throw over substance," says Russell in *Analysis of Matter*, " we preserve the causal chain, substituting the unity of a causal process for material identity. Thus the persistence of substance is replaced by the persistence of causal laws, which is, in fact, the criterion by which the supposed material identity was recognized. We thus preserve everything that there was reason to suppose true, and reject only a piece of unfruitful metaphysics."

Russell's theory of causation is difficult. He seems to regard it as invariable sequence—a view which is open to several objections. He has also declared that the term " cause " is not needed in advanced science. He rejects the idea of compulsive causes but retains the sequential chain.

The details of his theory must be sought in his more serious works. " The aim of physics, consciously or unconsciously, has always been to discover what we may call the causal skeleton of the world. It is perhaps surprising that there should be such a skeleton, but physics seems to prove that there is, particularly when taken in conjunction with the evidence that percepts are determined by the physical character of their stimuli. . . . We know of no laws as to when a quantum transaction will take place, or a radio-active atom will break down. We know fairly well what will happen *if* anything happens, and we know statistical averages, which suffice to determine macroscopic phenomena. . . . Perhaps the electron jumps when it likes ; perhaps the minute phenomena in the brain, which make all the difference to mental phenomena, belong to the region where physical laws no longer determine definitely what must happen. This, of course, is merely a speculative possibility ; but it interposes a veto upon materialistic dogmatism."

This passage shows the difference between Realism and the subjective theories which are now fashionable. Russell holds that there is no half-way house between Solipsism and Realism. The belief in an external world is necessary, he argues, for science, but it rests on a belief in causation and induction. He agrees that this foundation has not been justified in theory, but he points to its merits in practice.

" We cannot escape from the solipsist position without bringing in induction and causality, which are still subject to the doubts resulting from Hume's sceptical criticism. Since, however, all science rests upon induction and causality, it seems justifiable, at least pragmatically, to assume that, when properly employed, they can give at least a probability." (*Analysis of Matter*.)

Neutral Monism

At times Russell's epistemological views recall Berkeley's. Thus he regards the everyday world as a construction from percepts. He sometimes writes—perhaps because he enjoys the flavour of paradox—as though a construction is equivalent to a logical fiction, but he clearly regards the external world as a necessary inference. The originality of Russell's view is that he regards percepts and physical events as substantially the same. He is as opposed as Whitehead to the Cartesian dualism of mind and matter.

Like Hume, he denies that there is a substantial ego. He carries his war against metaphysical substance to the uttermost extreme. There is no " I," which owns mental states ; there are just the states, the events we call percepts. Thus (an echo from Leibniz, with a big difference) the whole of the perceived universe is inside our heads, quite literally inside our skulls. All we are acquainted with are percepts. And percepts are mental events. A physical object can be analysed into a string of events; and even a mind is no more than a bundle of events. To sum up:

" What has been thought of as a particle will have to be thought of as a series of events. The series of events that replaces the particle has certain important physical properties, and therefore demands our attention; but it has no more sub-stantiality than any other series of events that we might arbi-trarily single out. Thus ' matter ' is not a part of the ultimate material of the world, but merely a convenient way of collecting events into bundles. . . . While physics has been making matter less material, psychology has been making mind less mental. . . . The distinction of matter and mind came into philosophy from religion, although, for a long time, it seemed to have valid grounds. I think that both matter and mind are merely convenient ways of grouping events. Some single events, I should admit, belong only to material groups, but others belong to both kinds of groups, and are therefore at once mental and material." (*History of Western Philo-sophy*.)

Russell calls his theory Neutral Monism, which is perhaps not an altogether happy name because it suggests a doctrine of substance that he has spent much time in undermining. It would be equally misleading to call it either Idealism or Materialism. Professor Broad has criticized the theory that mind consists of percepts on the ground that feelings are not percepts, and that Russell makes much of feelings. But however much or little may survive of Neutral Monism, there can be no doubt that Russell has carried out a great part of his avowed programme " to eliminate Pythagoreanism from the principles of mathematics, and to combine empiricism with an interest in the deductive parts of human knowledge."

Logical Positivism

The influence of Russell has been enormous, and a more radical turn was given to analytical empiricism by his pupil, Ludwig Wittgenstein, a young architect who became successor to G. E. Moore at Cambridge.   For a time Wittgenstein was a member of a group that was formed in Vienna to discuss the sort of problems raised by Frege, Hilbert, Mach, Peano, and Russell.   This was known as the Vienna Circle, and started in 1923 under Moritz Schlick.   Few of the members were professional philosophers.

Schlick was a physicist, Hahn a mathematician, Otto Neurath a sociologist, Philip Frank a physicist.   One of the most influential members of the group was Carnap, though the movement received its strongest impetus from an astonishing book published by Wittgenstein in 1922, *Tractatus Logico-Philosophicus*.

The Vienna Circle called themselves, at first, Logical Positivists.   They deviated from the Cambridge analysts. Neurath and Carnap propounded the thesis of Radical Physicalism.   This has received many modifications, and after the war —central Europe having proved unfavourable to philosophic meditation—the group came to life again, with renewed vigour, in the United States, where Logical Positivism was re-named Logical Empiricism.

Logical Positivism won the wrong sort of notoriety by appearing to dismiss the objections of its opponents, the systems of all metaphysicians from Plato onwards, the objects of religious belief and any idea of right and wrong, as " nonsense."   It was certainly good clean fun, and young iconoclasts made the most of it.   Logical Positivism became fashionable among people quite incapable of understanding that " nonsense " was a technical term.   It would have been less misleading to have described some of the propositions objected to as " non-significant," or " without sense-content."   Inevitably the Logical Positivists had soon to distinguish between nonsense and " important " nonsense, between what is *unsinnig* (senseless) and what is useful but without sense (*sinnlos*), such as tautologies and contradictions.

Broadly speaking, Logical Positivism illustrates the transition from the sort of question raised by Locke—How much do we know ?—to the question, What do we mean ? The ancients asked what the world was made of ; the moderns ask what language is made of, or, more accurately, What are the constituents of propositions ? The early empiricists made a good beginning when they said that words were signs ; but when you analyse a sentence it becomes evident that some of the words it contains are not signs standing for sense-data. Language is not, on the face of it, a set of hieroglyphics, however it might have begun. Some account must therefore be given of those signs which do not simply represent experiences.

Most Logical Positivists dislike the term " experience." It has psychological associations. They prefer the more neutral word " facts." On the relation between facts and the verbal signs which stand for them the movement split.

Wittgenstein held that sentences are pictures of facts. We cannot express the relation between what is symbolized and the symbol, because to do so would violate this definition of a sentence, but we can *see* it. By using a different notation we can *see* that $II + II = IIII$.

All sensible propositions can be reduced to elementary propositions, just as you reduce a compound like water to hydrogen and oxygen, then to molecules, atoms, and finally to electrons and protons. These elementary propositions represent ultimately simple facts, atomic facts as it were. Thus the universe is a totality of atomic facts ; it is not, as organic theories claim, a whole of internally related events.

And so, to test the truth of a proposition, you must see whether its constituents (which can be obtained by analysing it) correspond to atomic facts, or what used to be called particulars. All verification consists in doing this. It consists in setting the linguistic atoms, if you like, beside the atoms of experience, the atomic facts. On the other hand, the procedure of philosophies of organism must be to seek, with Spinoza, coherence rather than correspondence.

For Wittgenstein the meaning of a proposition consists in the method of its verification. Propositions that seem to have a meaning and yet which cannot conceivably be verified are tautologies. They are more or less elaborate ways of saying the same thing in other words. All the laws of logic, all so-called necessary truths, are tautologies.

The laws of logic are not derived from experience, as empiricists like Mill believed. They are not synthetic but analytic, in the Kantian sense. They are rules of symbolism, not features of the universe. It follows that every attempt to deduce facts from logical principles, from supposed necessary truths, is tautologous. Mathematical deduction is also tautologous. If we were sufficiently intelligent we would be able to see that the whole of mathematics follows from certain principles.

Metaphysics, therefore, is to be rejected. It is really a sort of playing with words. It gives us no information whatever. It pretends to give information, and so it consists largely of pseudo-sentences—i.e., sentences without genuine significance, because they are intrinsically incapable of verification.

Wittgenstein claims to have given a rigorous proof that whatever can be established by purely logical methods can tell us nothing about empirical facts; and because of its sweeping consequences this is perhaps the most important part of his philosophy. The gist of the argument is that the only way in which logic applies to the world is that it shows how different modes of expression may convey the same sense. Logic provides the rules for translating one proposition into another.

Consider, for example, some typical metaphysical statements : " To be is to be perceived," " The real is the rational and the rational the real," " Pure Being and Pure Nothing are the same." Now either these statements are just repeating an assertion in different words or they are telling us something new. If they provide a basis for deduction, then something is being deduced from a complex concept—which must in any case entail all the simple concepts of which it is composed.

" How do you *know* what you are telling me ? " is a reasonable question to put to any philosopher.   The empiricist replies that in the last resort he can indicate how complex propositions can be reduced to elementary ones, and that these can be shown to correspond to facts of experience.   That is the only sort of information he can give.   It is, of course, merely scientific information.   It does not profess to take us behind the scenes of reality.

The metaphysician, on the other hand, is not satisfied with empirical concepts.   He claims to have a superior method of discovering truth—either by pure intuition or by deduction from propositions that are absolutely certain.   To which the empiricist answers : " Any such information must be expressed in language.   It is therefore open to the objection that any sentences that can be devised are either tautologies, or else verifiable, or else meaningless."

As Carnap puts it : " Metaphysicians cannot avoid making their propositions non-verifiable, because if they made them verifiable, the decision about the truth or falsehood of their doctrines would depend upon experience and therefore belong to the region of empirical science.   This consequence they wish to avoid, because they pretend to teach knowledge which is of a higher level than that of empirical science.   Thus they are compelled to cut all connection between their propositions and experience ; and precisely by this procedure they deprive them of any sense."   (*Philosophy and Logical Syntax.*)

The practical rule, " If this statement is significant it can be tested," has led some Logical Empiricists to find affinities with American Pragmatists and Instrumentalists.   As long ago as 1878 Charles Peirce said that the meaning of a statement was the practical effects it might have.   If a change of words makes no *practical* difference, the change tells us nothing.

As William James put it, " theories thus become instruments, not answers to enigmas."   According to Dewey and Bridgman scientific laws should be regarded as intellectual instruments which we use in our active exploration of the world.   To say that Newton's law of gravitation is true is to say that it can be applied successfully; so long as that could be done, it *was* true. There is no inconsistency in saying that Newton's law *was* true and that Einstein's law is *at present* true.

The Positivist account looks more like Pragmatism than it really is. It is designed to preserve the concept of " truth " and yet at the same time to overcome the difficulties about induction which Hume raised and Mill failed to solve. The thesis is that laws are not " true " when practically useful, as Pragmatists avow, but useful in so far as they yield true propositions. Laws are models—propositional functions—from which directives can be formed.

The old problem of arguing from the particular to the general does not arise. According to Schlick : " The relations between reality and ourselves frequently stand in sentences which have the grammatical form of assertions but whose essential sense consists in the fact that they are directions for possible acts."

The Principle of Verifiability has been toned down since it was first enunciated. It is plain that complete verifiability is seldom possible. And the more we move away from the metaphysical idea of certainty, the more necessary it becomes to discover what we mean by probability. This, however, is a problem that is far from being solved.

Wittgenstein so restricted the meaning of significance that he had to admit that his own thesis was " nonsense." He claimed that " the result of philosophy is not a number of ' philosophical propositions ' but to make propositions clear." Accordingly, he had to confess : " My propositions are elucidatory in this way : he who understands me finally recognizes them as senseless, when he has climbed out through them, on them, over them. (He must so to speak throw away the ladder after he has climbed up on it.) He must surmount these propositions ; then he sees the world rightly. Whereof one cannot speak, thereof one must be silent."

Another apparently self-strangulating course was taken by those who wished to forbid all reference to the factual world and confine the discussion within the sphere of language. The safest procedure was felt to be to confine the problem to that of transforming one set of expressions into another. But this was not a very bracing atmosphere for the scientific investigator.

The most recent trend has been an endeavour to show that all sciences are united by a common language. Just as chemistry is being reduced to physics, so, it is argued, it may be possible to effect a complete reduction of the laws of the various sciences to a unitary set of basic laws. " Reduction," of this sort, remarks Feigl, is to be contrasted with the " seduction " of metaphysics.

Thus, quite apart from vitalistic and spiritualistic theories, there is an important distinction between reductive Materialism on the one hand, and emergent Materialism on the other. As Russell has tried to show, reductive Materialism is not rendered invalid by the rejection of mechanism. But although it can be made compatible with the new physics, its psychological affinities with Behaviourism make it seem to many rather less respectable.

Like Hume and Russell, Logical Positivists must regard the substantial " I " as a pseudo-concept, because a pure ego has no empirical qualities. We cannot describe the experience of ourselves as the subject ; when we try to do so we are confronted with an object. There is obviously a vicious regress. But if we substitute physical terms for the subjective terms of psychology we can scarcely avoid Behaviourism. This would not dismay Russell ; but Dr. Broad, for example, who is no enemy of empiricism, classes Behaviourism among " theories so silly that only very learned men would have thought of them."

The point is this. Suppose I say I am thirsty. To reduce that to an empirical, non-metaphysical statement I merely assert " Now, thirst." The " I " is dropped out. It is regarded as a mere grammatical convenience. But how, on this basis, is it possible for me to tell someone else, or for him to tell me, that I am, or he is, thirsty ? All that can be done, according to Carnap, is to describe behaviour—because if we restrict ourselves to the physical language we cannot talk about private feelings. The solution advanced is to regard what a man says, or the state of his body (if it can be examined) as equivalent

N

(translatable into) the usual sentence about his subjective feelings.

The actual subjective feeling of Smith, for example, when he is thirsty, is known only to himself. It cannot be communicated. All we can communicate is the fact that Smith *says* he is thirsty or *says* that he is angry ; and this means that he is in a certain bodily, and so verifiable condition.

Once again, the argument has an appearance of triviality. Yet, if it is sound, it has the most revolutionary consequences. For it not merely disposes of the soul, it wipes out the mind and what we ordinarily call the self.

This is more than the familiar reduction of mind to physical brain, as the following illustration will show : The ordinary view of language as a set of signs requires (*a*) what is signified, (*b*) the sign, and (*c*) the interpreter of the sign, as signifying. Some Logical Positivists accept (*a*) and (*b*), some eliminate (*a*) and all reject (*c*).

Protesting against over-emphasis on the purely reductive aspect of analysis, Prof. C. I. Lewis writes : " The analysis of any immediately presented X must always interpret this X in terms of constant relations to other things—to Y and Z. Such end-terms of analysis—Y and Z—will not in general be temporal or spatial constituents of X but may be anything which is in constant correlation with it. It is as if one should deny the existence of colours because for purposes of exact investigation the colours must be defined as frequencies of vibratory motion." (*Mind and the World Order*.)

The Logical Positivist would probably answer that a sentence containing the word " colour " and a sentence containing the phrase " frequencies of vibratory motion," are different ways of saying the same thing. To say that a man's brain is in a certain state and to say that he is thinking is to make statements that can be substituted for one another without remainder. Such statements are " equipollent." The term " synonymous " must be kept for tautologies.

But by this time the reader will have become hardened to the startling claims that philosophers make. Now change is abolished, now permanence; now mind, now matter. This or that familiar interpretation has gone, and finally there is no one left to interpret anything. Looking back on all the various things that have made their positively last appearance—and turned up for a repeat performance in some other guise—can we be confident that even the metaphysician has left the stage for ever? If he does dare to reappear I think he will have to show some quite new tricks.

USEFUL REFERENCES

Our Knowledge of the External World, by Bertrand Russell; 1914.
Introduction to Mathematical Philosophy, by Bertrand Russell; 1919.
The Analysis of Mind, by Bertrand Russell; 1921.
The Analysis of Matter, by Bertrand Russell; 1927.
Inquiry into Meaning and Truth, by Bertrand Russell; 1940.
The Philosophy of Bertrand Russell, Library of Living Philosophers,
    V; 1946.
Philosophical Studies, by G. E. Moore; 1922.
Tractatus Logico-Philosophicus, by Ludwig Wittgenstein; 1922.
Pragmatism, by William James; 1907.
The Philosophy of "As If," by H. Vaihinger, Eng. trs.; 1924.
Logic, The Theory of Inquiry, by John Dewey; 1938.
An Examination of Logical Positivism, by J. R. Weinberg; 1936.
Philosophy and Logical Syntax, by Rudolf Carnap; 1935.
The Logical Syntax of Language, by Rudolf Carnap; 1937.
The Foundations of Empirical Knowledge, by A. J. Ayer; 1940.
The Logic of Modern Physics, by P. W. Bridgman; 1928.

CHAPTER THIRTEEN

The Debate Continues

BEFORE trying to sum up, I propose to mention two other recent contributions that bring into sharp focus the sort of questions to which answers are still being sought. The development of physics has led some physicists to adopt what is sometimes called Subjective Idealism.

Bertrand Russell has pointed out the difficulty of resting in a half-way house. We must either go the whole hog, he argues, and end up as Solipsists, or we must assume the validity of our inferences about unperceived events and accept the reality of the world and of our neighbours.

But who could possibly deny that other people exist? What man outside a lunatic asylum could declare that nothing exists but himself? For that is what the Solipsist *seems* to say.

Russell makes the sound point that our evidence for the existence of other people is the same as our evidence for the external world. If you do not believe that tables and chairs are real, you cannot believe that the objects that use them and make funny noises with their mouths are real.

On the other hand, Russell admits that Solipsism cannot be disproved. So here is a logical scandal. Solipsism seems laughable, absurd, outrageous—but no one can disprove it. A sufficiently bold thinker was therefore sure to come along and make things exceedingly awkward for those philosophers who felt that at last they were sorting things out very nicely.

A Modern Solipsist

In his 1936 Lowell Lectures, *Through Science to Philosophy*, Professor H. Dingle writes as follows : " The judgment which is usually passed on Solipsism is that it is logically irrefutable but intrinsically absurd, and may therefore be ignored. But if absurdity is logically irrefutable, what becomes of philosophy ? . . . Moreover, to say that Solipsism is logically irrefutable is to express the fact far too mildly. It is not merely logically irrefutable ; it is obviously true. . . . Anything that is not in my consciousness cannot be conceived by me, and can have no part (not *should* have no part, but *can* have no part) in my philosophy."

The reader who has followed me thus far through the twisting maze will not, I hope, be dazed by this apparent defiance of common sense. He will be prepared for an ingenious discussion about the meaning of the words " reality," " external," " consciousness," " my."

He will remember that Dr. Johnson was wrong when he kicked a stone to disprove Immaterialism. He will not, therefore, suppose that the fact that he is arguing with a Solipsist disproves Solipsism. He will recall, too, that Leibniz and Descartes accepted the solipsistic starting-point, and got themselves out of their difficulties by metaphysical arguments.

In the past, whenever a philosopher got into serious trouble, he could always extricate himself by the appeal to God. It is significant of a great change that the contemporary philosopher appears to pull himself out of the quicksands by his own braces.

In an earlier book, *Science and Human Experience*, Professor Dingle defined science as " the rational correlation of experiences common to all normal people." He has since found it necessary to amend this definition because " normal people " are a part of his experience. To get down to fundamentals they must not be taken for granted.

After quoting definitions of science by Einstein and others, which treat it as the rational correlation of experiences, Dingle says that this " specifies a process occurring in our consciousness ; that is, in fact, in the consciousness of the scientist, the thinker—in the last resort, in my consciousness, for it is only my consciousness that I am directly aware of and that can possibly be for me the scene of a mental operation. I have not reached rock-bottom until I have come down to the solipsistic level. Of course, I must not remain there. Normal people *are* part of my experience, and I must see that they, as well as the rest of what I find it convenient to call ' the external world,' receive their due in the building which is to be erected."

Dingle takes, as the primary elements of consciousness, experience and reason. What we ordinarily call the external world is a rational correlation of our sensations, emotions, etc. These are experiences, and their correlation into bits of matter, people, and so on is the world of reason. What you and I would regard as " Professor Dingle " is not given to us in experience but constructed rationally out of the experiences which we call seeing him, hearing him. So, to Dingle, is the person he speaks of as " myself," but a distinction must be drawn between " myself " and the subjective " I," which can also be referred to as reason. " When I speak of ' I and my consciousness,' then it is to be understood that ' I ' represents the thinker, ' my consciousness ' the aggregate of things of which thought is possible."

We cannot ever reach the thinker, in *this* sense. As soon as we talk about him (or he talks about himself) the thinker is objectified and becomes an object to a remoter thinker. To try and catch the latter is as impossible as catching your shadow. This is not the thinker which the psychologist studies. The psychologist studies part of the aggregate of things in the field of consciousness.

Dingle expresses this as lucidly as anyone can. " My subjective ' I,' ever at the present and continuously experiencing, has its experience automatically petrified and projected as memory into the field of consciousness by the unceasing action of time. In that field, through the agency of its timeless faculty of reason, it can work its will on memory, which it either apprehends as discrete atoms or breaks up into such atoms as the first stage in the formation of a completely rationalised system. The subsequent stages constitute the progress of philosophy, including that of science."

The Atoms of Logic

It should be explained that the atoms referred to are units of experience and not physical atoms. Reason forms four classes of concepts in its activity of correlating and subsuming atomic experiences. The latter are grouped into logical molecules, which in the scientific world are groups of similar experiences, and in the ordinary world of common sense, physical objects. The atomic experience which is a blue patch is grouped by the physicist into the molecule of colour. To establish connections between the atoms in the molecules themselves, reason invents postulates. Light is such a postulate—so are space, time, mass, and force. In addition to molecules and postulates, reason employs hypotheses and laws of Nature.

A certain class of hypothesis is a pseudo-atom or pseudo-molecule, which may be transformed into an actual atom of experience. "A familiar example of a pseudo-molecule was the planet Neptune, which, before its discovery, was compounded of a colour, a mass, a shape, and so on, none of which had been actually experienced. It was created by reason to serve as an intermediary in connecting the two molecules known as the planet Uranus and the sun. . . . Neptune was accordingly 'created' by reason as a pseudo-molecule, and subsequent observation converted it into an actual one."

It is clear that this kind of approach is a development of the atomism implicit in Locke, Berkeley, and Hume. Atomic experiences are a modern formulation of "ideas." Out of them we form physical objects.

Take, for example, two common-sense physical objects, a billiard ball and a piece of sugar. "The first is a spatio-temporal association of a red colour, round shape, hard feeling, horizontal movement and such things; and the second is a similar but differently located association of a white colour, hard feeling, cubical outline, sweet taste and so on." But these associations are not of much use to the scientist. He makes a different set of associations.

" I put the horizontal movement of the disintegrated billiard ball with the perpetual rest of the disintegrated piece of sugar, and form a general concept called ' motion ' which includes them as examples.   Similarly, I take the red colour of the one and the white colour of the other, and make them into a molecule covered by the concept ' light.' "   By elaborating this process we get sound, magnetism, electricity, and the laws of these fields.   " We form laws of motion but no laws of sugar. One of the most fruitful causes of misunderstanding of science is failure to recognize this fact, which is obvious when it is once mentioned.   When a new phenomenon appears—say a new kind of beetle—it is immediately dissected into qualities which are distributed among the various sciences.   The characteristics of its nervous system are alloted to biology ;   mechanics takes charge of its locomotion ;   optics looks after the iridescence of its outer covering and so on."

Dingle, therefore, takes his stand with the Logical Empiricists against organic theories.   Where he mainly seems to differ from them is in regard to the subjective " I ".   " The Logical Positivists' proscription of everything that is not verifiable," he writes, " is an unsuccessful attempt to express the truth that what is subjective cannot at the time be objective without becoming nonsense. . . . But the Logical Positivist fails to observe, first, that the subjective element is as necessary to consciousness as the objective ;   and secondly, that while subjective (metaphysical) entities, such as the self, cannot as subjective entities be discussed, we can, by our faculty of being able to travel along an infinitely regressive consciousness, objectify them and make them objects of contemplation by a remote subjective self."

For the Logical Positivist any proposition in which " I " occurs is, strictly speaking, nonsense.   We make use of such propositions for convenience, just as we talk of sunrise and sunset.   Indeed, the more ruthless Positivists eliminate both " I " and the external world and are left merely with sentences. Wittgenstein takes refuge in a form of linguistic solipsism.

He agrees that other people are configurations of the facts of " my experience," but he insists that strictly speaking I mus

not talk of *my* experience.   " The thinking, presenting subject ;
there is no such thing.   If I wrote a book ' The World as I
Found It ' I should have to report therein on my body and say
which members obey my will and which do not, etc.   This then
would be a method of isolating the subject or, rather, of showing
that in an important sense there is no subject : that is to say, of
it alone in this book, mention could not be made.   The subject
does not belong to the world but is a limit of the world.   Here
we see that Solipsism strictly carried out coincides with pure
Realism, the ' I ' in Solipsism shrinks to an extensionless point
and there remains the reality co-ordinated with it."

This amounts to saying that what Solipsism means cannot be
expressed in language.

Experience and Knowledge

An alternative view suggested by Professor C. I. Lewis in
Mind and the World Order, a most important book, seeks to
avoid Solipsism.   Whereas Dingle follows Berkeley in affirming
that we have introspective knowledge of self (though we cannot
communicate it), Lewis follows Hume.   He takes a pragmatic
view of knowledge, but he, too, stresses that the concepts we
employ are not fixed categories, but creations of reason.

He starts with the empiricist's dictum that the proper subject-
matter of philosophy is experience.   " Everyone can be his own
philosopher because we interpret what we already know."
What do we already know and what do we mean by interpretation ?

Raw experience is " the given."   But we cannot dignify
awareness with the name of knowledge until we have sorted out
this raw material into some kind of order.   We cannot classify
and arrange until we have invented some scheme of classification.   To do this we must invent abstract terms (concepts),
and, because we must possess them before we can apply them,
they are *a priori*.   But, unlike the Kantian *a priori*, they are not
fixed ; they are more like definitions.

For example, we have an experience which could be described
as seeing a pool fringed by palms in the middle of a desert.

Is it real or mirage ?   That is simply a question of classification. We invent the term " reality " and define it in such a way that what does not fit is " mirage."

Such concepts are not eternal categories.   They are made by mind and can be changed by mind.   Indeed some do change and some are dropped altogether.   New concepts may have to be invented to account for new experiences.   To classify experiences of hypnotism, etc., we now find the concept of the Unconscious useful.   Every enlargement of experience demands new concepts.

We play a sort of game of " animal, vegetable, or mineral " with what is given in experience.   What is orderly we call " real," so there is simply no sense in demanding that the real should be orderly.   The category " unreal " is a temporary pigeon-hole for otherwise unclassified experiences.

" Things exist for our apprehension as certain sequences of possible experiences, of which given presentations are probable indices."   For knowledge to be possible, therefore, the possibilities of further experience should not be unlimited.   " Knowledge " is not just bare, immediate awareness ; it is the result of applying a conceptual scheme to the objects of which we are aware.

We devise this scheme in advance of knowledge.   We decide whether to play " animal, vegetable, or mineral " or some other game.   We classify some facts as " physical," others as " mental," but what we do is in no way final.   Such judgments are probable only.   Laws are empirical generalizations from certain recurrent correlations of experience which are usually classified as " things."   Every sequence of experience must show statistical stabilities of some sort and enable us to give probable predictions.

We interpret our experience in the interests of action.   " If I do this—then so and so will probably happen."   We set up hypotheses and test them.   We cannot obtain complete verifiability, but it is sufficient for practical purposes to know that the roof will not fall on our heads.

Because we are active beings, the world is bigger than

experience ; but knowledge is not merely a relation of the individual mind to an external object such that the existence of other minds is irrelevant. The categories we devise as guides to action are partly social products. " Our common understanding and our common world may be in part created in response to our need to act together and to comprehend one another."

Has Philosophy Progressed

It is not my task, fortunately, to decide among the various theories that I have described. If the reader feels that at this stage I ought to produce some final scheme that will clear up the perplexities I have dealt with, I fear that he will be disappointed. But I have not concealed my view that the metaphysical method was a mistake, and so I can at least express the opinion that all systems constructed on the basis of deductive Rationalism must be rejected. The more fruitful line seems to me to have been the empirical tradition derived from Locke.

If that is correct we can narrow down the philosophies which need claim our present attention very considerably. We can rule out the system-builders—though that does not mean that everything they said can be ignored. I shall have done my task badly if I have left the impression that we have little to learn from those massive intellects who tried to see the universe clearly and to see it whole. They swept away vast jungles of misunderstanding. No one can read Leibniz and Spinoza and Kant, to name but three, without finding an illumination on the present-day formulation of the perennial problems of man and the cosmos. Although they attempted the impossible, they achieved much that was permanently valuable.

My contention has been that, despite appearances to the contrary, philosophy has made progress, albeit of an unusual kind. Its most solid progress has not been in answering questions, but in propounding *better* questions. If it is asked whether philosophy has made any discoveries, I think we may reply that it has discovered what it is doing.

Let us glance back briefly at our starting-point. The

Ionians began it all by asking, What is the world made of ? By their discovery of reason they implied that there was an order, not visible to the naked eye, behind the haphazard occurrences of everyday life. The first inquirers, therefore, were led on to ask what was implied by an order of nature. Philosophy had emerged from a religious background, and some doctrines seemed as certain as the facts of ordinary observation. The natural answer was that an order of nature implied an ordering Mind—God.

If nature is orderly, and God made it so, we can apply reason to the concept of God. It used to be thought that we could discover something about the nature of God as well as about the nature of Nature by reasoning. I have shown where this led.

For two thousand years the double inquiry went on. The majority of philosophers, until the seventeenth century, seemed to find speculations about God even more fascinating than speculations about nature. The pre-eminence of theology was not seriously threatened in the period between the collapse of Alexandrian science and the Renaissance.

The attempt to answer the questions of the Ionians gave rise to a variety of theories that may be classed under two headings, (a) Materialism, (b) Idealism. As far as possible I have avoided this sort of classification because I do not think it is very helpful. The most fundamental difference between philosophers is in their method of approach. Yet Materialism and Idealism may agree about method but differ in the solutions put forward. There are, for example, metaphysical Materialists and empirical Idealists.

The Materialists said that the world was made of atoms. Everything that happened could be described in terms of matter in motion. To maintain this it had to be supposed that the world disclosed by the senses was somehow delusive. The reality was the atoms that could not be seen, not the objects that people saw.

Materialism of this sort was just as much an affront to common sense as Berkeley's Immaterialism. Secondary qualities were given a place in mind—and mind became a dumping ground for whatever spoilt the neatness of the picture.

It was partly to meet this situation that new kinds of Materialism were formulated. Both Emergent and Dialectical Materialism claimed to answer a difficulty about secondary qualities, which was seen to be also involved with the deeper problems of change. It seemed hardly possible to believe that the only sort of change that occurred was change of position by atoms as alike as two peas.

Mechanical Materialism was a bold simplification. Logically it rested on a dubious, metaphysical view of substance. Its decline, however, was due to the fact that philosophers were driven out of the foothold on physical science that they struggled hard to keep.

Mechanism was compatible, oddly enough, with Deism, but not with the new physics. Emergent Materialism is clearly incompatible with Deism, while Dialectical Materialism is aggressively Atheistic.

The Shifting of the Problem

It will be noticed, however, that none of these theories manages to banish what may be called the mysteriousness or, better still, the awkwardness of the universe. The Mechanist transfers it from matter to God, if he is a Deist, or to mind if he is not. The Emergent Materialist transfers it to an unborn God. The Dialectical Materialist transfers it to eternally self-moving matter. An alternative to solutions of this sort is Idealism.

By Idealism I mean all theories that regard matter as derivative. It is impossible to use these terms with complete consistency. A Mechanical Materialist who is also a Deist is an Idealist if he regards the material world as a creation of God, provided he regards God as pure Mind. But there is a practical convenience in classifying the various philosophical answers on this basis.

Clearly there have been many philosophers who regarded

material objects as in some sense *thoughts*—either as complexes of universals or thoughts in the mind of God or thoughts in the mind of man. But we cannot examine the rival merits of Idealism and Materialism for long without realizing that the old question, " *What* is the world made of ? " is not fundamental. We are obliged to ask ourselves, " *How* can we find out what the world is made of ? " and finally, " What do we *mean* by ' finding out ' ? "

When we examine the manner in which we can conduct the inquiry we find that there are at least two obvious methods. We can consider the ideas in our heads and ask what they imply, what we can deduce from them ; or we can observe what happens and generalize. We could deduce a lot of information from our ideas if we could be sure that these ideas were true. Metaphysical inquiry demands a belief that we can have a direct intuition into the nature of reality.

No one, of course, would be so foolish as to deny that such a thing is possible. Some mathematical and scientific discoveries have come in a flash of intuition. But scientific intuitions have always been tested afterwards. They are accepted because they have survived repeated experiments, not because they were first thought of on top of a bus.

If our concepts give us a direct insight into reality—as Hegel believed—it is evident that the metaphysician has a different *kind* of knowledge from the scientist. He does not merely know certain abstract features of the universe. He knows it from the inside, as he knows his own toothache. Pragmatists and empiricists make no such claims.

Pragmatists regard scientific knowledge as little more than a set of rules for our guidance when we have to act. The rules are the best available, but from time to time they may have to be seriously modified. Once we leave the private data of immediate experience we say good-bye to certainty and enter what Locke called " the twilight of probability."

The sharpest distinction between the metaphysical and the empirical method is seen in the treatment of concepts. For Hegel a material object—say, a sparrow—was merely a complex of abstract ideas. To analyse it is to show that it consists of universals.

For an empiricist, universals are symbolical devices for grouping particulars. The sparrow can be analysed into sense-data ; bundles of sense-data can be re-grouped and handed over to various departments for study—the colour and weight to the physicist, other groupings to the chemist, still others to the biologist. The empiricist invents new concepts ; he invents Mass and Inertia, for example. But although the task may be difficult, such concepts can be broken down again finally into sensible constituents, or shown to be functions of them.

From this point of view we can see that a stage is reached when the problem of the philosopher is not about the *world*, but about *experience*. Immediate awareness is contrasted with an orderly system of interpretations. The " world," as the object of anything worthy of the name of knowledge, is a rational construction. We devise a conceptual scheme, we keep on improving it, and we sort out our experiences and connect them to form a system within this scheme of concepts.

Something like this is so widely admitted nowadays that I think we may almost regard it as a piece of territory conquered by the philosopher. Even Whitehead, who cannot be regarded as a pure empiricist, describes his aim as the search for a set of ideas in terms of which everything we experience can be interpreted. The other philosophers whom we have considered—Russell, the Logical Positivists, Dingle, and Lewis—also have a similar aim, though they might word it differently. It seems evident that they are all engaged in trying to devise a conceptual scheme, and that they regard themselves as a good deal freer than most of their predecessors to invent concepts.

This *freedom* is the note of contemporary thought. When the results are described as tentative or probable, or as working hypotheses, the emphasis is laid on our ignorance ; but from another point of view it draws attention to the important discovery that *a priori* truths are either about symbolism or are definitive.

As definitions, *a priori* concepts are devised with the object of constructing an orderly universe out of primitive experience. That, too, seems to be widely admitted. There are, of course, disagreements about details. If primitive experience is described as non-inferential knowledge, the construction may be regarded as inferred knowledge, and we are faced with the problem of the validity of inference, when it does more than generalize instances. In what sense, we then ask, are our constructions *true*?

Russell frankly assumes the validity of induction and the existence of causal laws. He writes : " In such cases, I shall allow myself to accept what seems necessary on pragmatic grounds, being content, as science is, if the results obtained are often verifiably true and never verifiably false. But wherever a principle is accepted on such grounds as these, the fact should be noted, and we should realize that there remains an intellectual problem, whether soluble or not." (*Analysis of Matter.*)

Lewis also accepts the pragmatic view, but Wittgenstein and Dingle boldly attempt to tackle the intellectual problem which, as Russell says, still remains. Wittgenstein tries to dispense altogether with unobserved entities. All agree that the constructions made as a result of ordering experience according to a scheme of concepts are dependent on primitive facts—that the entities of the world of reason must somehow be related to entities of the world of sense.

Whether concepts are best regarded as functions of sense-data or as abstractions that can be translated into protocol statements of the type " Red, now," is perhaps a question of taste. Similarly, the argument about Solipsism seems to me, at least, largely verbal. If the " I " cannot be described we cannot make valid propositions in which it occurs. We cannot discuss it. The sort of Solipsism which includes the world in " myself " and common sense rightly laughs at, is manifest nonsense ; the sort of Solipsism which tries to put the world inside brackets labelled " I " is inescapable, but the brackets represent the limit of what can be said. We must take care not to embarrass ourselves with an unknowable *Ding an sich* outside them.

However, all this is, in a sense, a family quarrel and should not be allowed to obscure the broad agreement and the solid results achieved by empiricism. It accounts more satisfactorily than any other school of philosophy for what science is doing, and if it leads us into difficult and technical and even astonishing discussions, that is because science becomes increasingly difficult, technical, and astonishing.

Philosophy and Life

In treating that aspect of philosophy which is an adventure of ideas, and in suggesting that it can be studied because of the simple pleasure it gives, I am very far from regarding it as an escape from life, an activity to be confined in Flaubert's Ivory Tower. But I certainly hold that it is a delightful pursuit, and I think that that is the psychological reason why individuals take so much trouble to study both science and philosophy. " The scientist does not study nature because it is useful to do so," wrote Henri Poincaré. " He studies it because he takes pleasure in it, and he takes pleasure in it because it is beautiful."

Can we say of a piece of reasoning that it is beautiful ? I think the elegance and simplicity of a logical demonstration can unquestionably give some people an æsthetic satisfaction akin to that derived from a work of art. The Greeks understood this, which is perhaps why they described philosophers as *lovers* of wisdom and truth.

Love is a strong word, but not, I think, too strong for a passion which scorns the harlotry of fantasy and demands that those dedicated to an austere beauty should be faithful even unto death. The love of truth—which must not be confused with love of certainty—has seldom made much appeal to religious minds. Without it, however, philosophy would have foundered in sterile scholasticism, and there would have been no science.

Science, with the transforming material power it gives us, is among the practical consequences of philosophy. There are other consequences with which I have no space to deal. And in the sphere of morals and religion it undoubtedly makes a

o

great difference whether our approach is metaphysical or empirical.

William James praises the philosopher who " turns away from abstraction and insufficiency, from verbal solutions, from bad *a priori* reasons, from fixed principles, closed systems and pretended absolutes and origins. He turns towards concreteness and adequacy, towards facts, towards action and towards power. That means the empiricist temper regnant and the rationalist temper sincerely given up. It means the open air and possibilities of nature, as against dogma, artificiality, and pretence of final truth." (*Pragmatism*, 1907.)

The empiricist is no doctrinaire who seeks to compel men to comply with his views. Unlike the metaphysician, he does not claim to possess knowledge that is certain and unshakable, and so he is a little less likely to persecute those who disagree with him. In their armchairs, metaphysicians do not seem able to do much harm, but when they inspire political action the result is invariably some form of despotism. If philosophers ever become kings it is to be hoped that they will be empiricists.

The intolerance of most religions is due to their arrogant claim of possessing certainty ; but it is not quite true to say that all religious teachers have been metaphysical in the bad sense.

It is said that some students once approached Buddha and complained that they were bewildered by the variety of doctrines taught by philosophers and did not know what to believe or how to act. In his reputed reply Buddha expressed what seems to me to be the essence of the empiricist attitude in words that could scarcely be bettered. He said : " Believe nothing on the faith of traditions, even though they have been held in honour for many generations, and in divers places. Do not believe a thing because many speak of it. Do not believe on the faith of the sages of the past. Do not believe what you have imagined, persuading yourself that a god inspires you. Believe nothing on the sole authority of your masters or priests. After examination, believe what you yourself have tested and found to be reasonable, and conform your conduct thereto."

USEFUL REFERENCES

Contemporary British Philosophy, Ed. by J. H. Muirhead, two vols.; 1924–25.
Through Science to Philosophy, by H. Dingle; 1936.
Mind and the World Order, by C. I. Lewis; 1929.
An Analysis of Knowledge and Valuation, by C. I. Lewis; 1946.
The Logic of Modern Physics, by P. W. Bridgman; 1928.
Critical Thinking : An Introduction to Logic and Scientific Method, by Max Black; 1946.

Glossary of Terms

[These definitions are intended as aids to understanding and are not to be taken as precise.]

ABSTRACTA are general or universal terms such as Beauty, Truth, Number, Equality.

ABSTRACTION is the logical process of isolating an aspect from the total object.

ANALYTIC describes a judgment in which the subject contains the predicate.

A PRIORI is a judgment independent of sense-impressions; non-empirical and universal.

A POSTERIORI refers to the sort of knowledge acquired by experience.

ATOMISM is the logical doctrine that there are certain basic, simple propositions from which other propositions are constructed. It is denied that all the facts in the universe are necessarily connected.

ATTRIBUTE is that which expresses the nature of a substance. In logic it is that which is predicated of the subject of a proposition.

CARTESIAN. The philosophy of Descartes.

CATEGORIES are the inescapable forms in which knowledge is presented. For Aristotle they were ultimate modes of being—viz., substance, quantity, quality, relation, place, time, position, etc. For Kant they were part of the apparatus of knowledge.

CONCEPT is a general or abstract term. Conception is knowledge of universals or abstracta, in contrast to perception as awareness of particulars.

CONNOTATION is the set of characteristics that belong to an object.

COHERENCE is a characteristic of a system in which every fact is related to every other fact.

CORRESPONDENCE THEORY OF TRUTH asserts that the truth of propositions depends on a one-one correspondence between the terms and facts.

COSMOLOGICAL ARGUMENT is a proof of the existence of a *First Cause* from series of causes; or sometimes of Necessary Being from Contingent Being.

DATUM is what is immediately given to the mind, the raw material of sense-impressions yet to be interpreted.

DEDUCTION is a type of inference from the general to the particular. The conclusion necessarily follows from the premises.

DENOTATION is the object to which a word applies.

DETERMINISM is the theory that everything that exists conforms to law.

DIALECTIC originally meant the process of argument by question and answer. For Hegel it became the law of the development of thought whereby the contradictions of thesis and antithesis are resolved in synthesis.

EMPIRICAL is what is derived from experience.

EPISTEMOLOGY is the theory of knowledge.

ESSENCE is the nature of a thing, that which makes it unique.

EXTENSION is physical space in contrast to the abstract space of mathematics. In logic the extension of an object is whatever it includes.

FORM has a variety of meanings. Traditionally, substantial form is what differentiates a thing from any other and determines its species or class; as opposed to accidental form. In modern logic, formal is that which is independent of meaning, such as a symbol.

IDEALISM is, broadly speaking, any philosophy opposed to Materialism. Metaphysical Idealism asserts that reality is mental or spiritual; epistemological Idealism regards ideas (the content of experience) as the data of knowledge.

IDEOLOGY is nowadays usually taken to mean the socially conditioned (and therefore impermanent), categories of thought.

IMMEDIATE is by direct awareness ; interpretations and scientific constructions are mediate.

INDUCTION is the process of generalizing from a set of observations.

INFERENCE is the process of passing from one or more propositions believed to be true to another proposition which seems to be implied.

INNATE IDEAS are those concepts believed to be inborn. Their existence was affirmed by Descartes and denied by Locke.

LOGISTICS is modern symbolic logic.

MECHANISM is the theory that all phenomena can be reduced to the laws of matter in motion.

METAPHYSICS is traditionally the science of Being or Ontology. Metaphysical knowledge is obtained by deduction from axioms and claims to be universal and certain in contrast to empirical knowledge, which claims only to be probable.

MODES are classes or categories in addition to True and False : viz., potential, actual, possible, necessary. For Spinoza a mode is " that which exists in, and is conceived through, something other than itself." Thus motion and rest are modes of Extension, which is an attribute of Divine Substance.

MONAD is an irreducible unit, the metaphysical counterpart of the scientific atom.

MONISM is the theory that there is but one fundamental substance.

NECESSARY is opposed to contingent, or what might have been otherwise, and it is applied to propositions whose truth can be certified on *a priori* or logical grounds.

NOMINALISM is the doctrine that universals are mere names ; the opposite view that they really exist was held by Plato and known in the Middle Ages as Realism.

NOUMENON is a Kantian term for the unknowable world of reality held to lie behind appearances, or phenomena.

OBJECTIVE refers to whatever exists independently of the knowing mind.

ONTOLOGICAL is sometimes used to distinguish the independently real from the subjective or epistemological object.

PANTHEISM is the theory that nothing truly exists except God.

PARTICULAR is individual as opposed to universal; or, in logic, a member of a class.

PERCEPTS are sometimes called particulars. They are sense-objects such as tables and chairs, trees and mountains.

PHENOMENA are appearances, in contrast to things-in-themselves, or noumena.

PLURALISM is the theory that reality is composed of many irreducible substances.

POSITIVISM is the theory that knowledge describes phenomena and that metaphysics is largely meaningless.

PRAGMATISM is the theory that the meaning and truth of a proposition depend on its consequences. If two propositions yield the same consequences they have the same meaning. Beliefs are for the purposes of action, and if that is successful the beliefs are " true."

PREDICATE is what asserts a quality of a subject. Thus, in " Socrates is mortal," Socrates is the subject and mortal the predicate.

PROPOSITION is a sentence which express a truth or falsehood.

RATIONALISM is the philosophical theory that the criterion of truth is intellectual, and not sensory; the chief exponents were Descartes, Leibniz, and Spinoza. Opposed to it are Empiricism and Positivism, with which, curiously enough, modern Rationalism has come to be associated. The word has changed its original meaning.

REALISM to-day means the theory that we have direct knowledge of an external world.

REPRESENTATIONALISM is the theory that the mind knows the external world through the mediation of ideas which represent objects.

SEMANTICS is the study of the relation of signs to the objects to which they are applicable.

SENSA are isolated sense-qualities.

SENSATIONALISM is the theory that knowledge is ultimately derived from sensations.

SOLIPSISM is an epistemological theory which takes the experiencing Self as the starting-point for all knowledge and regards the external world as a rational construction by the Self from the raw material of its experience.

SPECIES is a class included in a wider class, the genus.

SUBJECTIVE IDEALISM is less radical than Solipsism, though the latter may be included under this heading.

SUBSTANCE was identical with essence in Greek philosophy, though the Scholastics drew a distinction. Substance has been regarded as that which exists in itself and independently of another being ; the substratum supporting qualities ; the ultimate subject of predication.

SYNTHETIC is a type of judgment in which the predicate is not contained in the subject—in opposition to analytic.

TELEOLOGICAL means purposive. The belief in final causes is teleological.

TRANSCENDENT is the opposite of immanent. It is what is beyond possible experience. Transcendental philosophy is a name for Kantianism.

Table of Dates

B.C.

Thales, *c.* 624–546.
Anaximander, *c.* 610–546.
Anaximenes, *c.* 585–528.
Pythagoras, *c.* 571–497.
Heraclitus, *c.* 504–501.
Parmenides, *c.* 501–492.
Zeno of Elea, *c.* 464.
Anaxagoras, *c.* 500–428.
Empedocles, *c.* 484–424.
Democritus, *c.* 460–371.
Socrates, 469–399.
Plato, 427–348.
Aristotle, 384–322.
Epicurus, 341–270.
Zeno of Citium, 336–264.

A.D.

Plotinus, 205–220.
Augustine, 354–430.
Abélard, 1079–1142.
Maimonides, 1135–1204.
Aquinas, 1225–1274.
William of Occam, died 1349.
Bruno, 1548–1600.
Galileo, 1564–1642.
Hobbes, 1588–1679.
Locke, 1632–1714.
Spinoza, 1632–1677.

Newton, 1642–1727.
Leibniz, 1646–1716.
Berkeley, 1685–1753.
Voltaire, 1694–1778.
Lamettrie, 1709–1751.
Hume, 1711–1776.
Condillac, 1715–1780.
d'Holbach, 1723–1789.
Kant, 1724–1804.
Fichte, 1762–1814.
Hegel, 1770–1831.
Schopenhauer, 1788–1860.
Comte, 1798–1857.
J. S. Mill, 1806–1873.
Marx, 1818–1883.
Engels, 1820–1895.
Herbert Spencer, 1820–1903.
T. H. Huxley, 1825–1895.
Avenarius, 1843–1896.
C. S. Peirce, 1839–1914.
William James, 1842–1910.
F. H. Bradley, 1846–1924.
Henri Bergson, 1859–1941.
S. Alexander, 1859–1938.
John Dewey, 1859–   .
A. N. Whitehead, 1861–1948.
Lenin, 1870–1924.
Bertrand Russell, 1872–   .
C. I. Lewis, 1883–   .
R. Carnap, 1891–   .

INDEX

Abélard, 27
Absolute, the, 42, 84, 110, 116, 149
  Idea, the, 114, 118, 119
Abstraction, 68, 85, 110, 111, 150,
  156
Addison, 65
Agnosticism, 150
Alexander, Samuel, 161, 162
Analysis, logical, 167, 184
Analysis of Matter, The (Russell),
  141, 176, 198
Analytic judgment, 76, 77
Anaxagoras, 20
Anaximander, 13, 14
Antithesis, 113, 122
Appearance and Reality (Bradley),
  153
Apperception, 94
A priori, 80, 89, 98, 123, 143, 191,
  197
A posteriori, 90
Aristotle, 3, 6, 21, 23, 61, 65, 114
Aristotelian logic, 23, 24, 83, 111,
  169
Association of ideas, 75, 80, 85
Atomic theory, ancient, 19, 21
  modern, 163, 175, 176
Atheism, 43, 96, 136, 195
Avenarius, 146

Babylonia, 1, 13
Bacon, Francis, 31, 62, 86
Bacon, Roger, 27
Beauty, 21, 199
Becoming, 109, 113, 114, 152
Behaviourism, 34, 183
Bergson, 15, 151, 160, 171
Berkeley, 4, 5, 6, 118, 146
  and Hegel, 71, 103
  and Hume, 74, 75, 82
  theory of knowledge, 66–72
Bohr, 135
Bradley, 98, 120, 153
Bridgman, 181
Broad, C. D., 37, 171, 183
Bruno, 28
Buddha, 200

Cantor, 171
Carnap, R., 73, 178, 181, 183
Cassirer, 85
Categories, 89, 91, 92, 98, 192, 193
Caudwell, C., 121
Causation, 23, 73, 93, 142, 144
  Hegel on, 102, 142
  Hume on, 64, 73, 79
  Russell on, 80, 175, 198
  Whitehead on, 157, 158
Change, problem of, 14–16, 117,
  149–166
  Bergson on, 152
  dialectical, 107, 125, 128, 151
  as illusion, 18, 105
Chaos, 20, 86
Christianity Not Mysterious (Toland)
  65
Comte, 136
Concepts, 10, 45, 51, 67, 82, 84,
  175, 196
  connective, 88
  reality of, 76, 83, 84, 95, 103, 107
  scientific, 190, 191, 192, 197
  sensuous and non-sensuous, 83,
    89, 98, 103, 104
Concept of Nature (Whitehead), 157
Condillac, 60, 136
Contradiction, 40, 76, 77, 114, 126,
  127, 174
Cotes, Roger, 56
Crisis in Physics, The (Caudwell),
  132
Critique of Judgment (Kant), 87
Critique of Practical Reason (Kant),
  87
Critique of Pure Reason (Kant), 87,
  93

Dalton, 135
Darwin, 135, 151
Definition, 111, 112, 191
Defoe, 65
Deism, 136, 142, 150, 195
Democritus, 19, 22, 30
Descartes, 5, 28, 29, 118
  and cogito, 4, 33

Descartes and God, 40, 41, 43
  and innate ideas, 35, 83
  and method, 32, 35, 187
  and substance, 33, 34, 36, 42
Determinism, 36, 43, 139, 150
Dewey, J., 181
d'Holbach, 136
Dialectic, 113, 114, 119, 123, 128, 135
Dialectics of Nature (Engels), 121
Dingle, H., 186–191, 197, 198
Diogenes, 31
Driesch, 24
Dualism, 33, 36, 45
Duration, 160–162

EDDINGTON, 8
Efficient Cause, 23
Einstein, 50, 135, 146, 147, 158, 170, 182, 187
Egypt, 1, 13
Élan vital, 152
Eleatics, 18
Empedocles, 14
Empiricism, 18, 64, 143, 200
  methods of, 84, 142, 156
  and logic, 143, 171, 178, 180
  and Rationalism, 56, 76
Encyclopedists, 135, 136, 137
Engels, 121, 122, 124, 126, 127, 130, 131
Epicureans, 27
Essay Concerning Human Understanding, An (Locke), 52, 53
Event, 25, 158, 159, 160, 164, 170, 177
Evolution, 13, 18, 125, 151, 152, 153, 161
Ewing, A. C., 97
Existence, 9, 94, 96, 104, 106, 107, 168, 173
Experience, 9, 10, 72, 73, 98, 188, 189, 191, 197
Extension, 42, 71, 91

FARRINGTON, B., 121
Feigl, 183
Fichte, 135
Final cause, 23
First cause, 23, 102, 142
First Principles (Spencer), 151
Forms, 22, 23
Forms of intuition, 89
Formal cause, 23

Formal logic, 24
Frank, Philip, 178
Freewill, 37, 45, 96
Frege, 171, 178
Freud, 135
From Religion to Philosophy (Cornford), 7

GALILEO, 4, 27, 135, 169
  and Copernicus, 29, 32
  and experiments, 30
  and Hobbes, 31
Genus, 54, 108, 111, 112, 113
Given, the, 10, 86, 97, 191
God, 150, 195
  existence of, 28, 35, 40, 60, 95, 96, 136, 142
  finite, 154, 164, 165, 195
  mind of, 14, 20, 194
  as substance, 42, 45
  as Supreme Monad, 49

HAHN, 178
Haldane, J. B. S., 121
Hegel, 5, 15, 100–116, 169
  and Berkeley, 103
  and dialectic, 108, 109, 113, 123, 127
  and history, 119, 132
  and Kant, 98, 101
  and the limit to Knowledge, 95
  and Materialism, 118
Hegelians, 119, 120
Heraclitus, 2, 4, 14, 15, 16, 22, 31, 117
Hesiod, 13, 20
Hilbert, 178
History of Western Philosophy (Russell), 152, 171
Hobbes, 27, 31, 32, 62, 86
Homer, 13
Hook, Sidney, 127
Hume, 5, 6, 60, 84, 85, 92, 176
  and causation, 64, 73, 79
  and impressions, 75, 80, 174
  and induction, 78, 79, 147, 182
  and logical analysis, 174
  and the self, 63, 78
Hypothesis, 123, 137, 138, 139, 140, 192

IDEALISM, 21, 49, 194, 195
  objective, 110, 118, 122, 170
  subjective, 4, 20, 50, 63, 187

Ideology, 110, 118, 122, 170
Immaterialism, 69, 187, 194
Immediate, 114
Immortality, 95, 96
Indeterminate, the, 14
Indian Philosophy (Dasgupta), 78
Induction, 78, 79, 80, 81, 140–145,
    176, 182
Innate Ideas, 34, 45, 51, 58, 67
*Inquiry Concerning Human Under-
    standing* (Hume), 74
Instrumentalism, 181
Intuition, 40, 60, 72, 80, 88, 196
Ionians, 1–3, 11, 16, 61, 70, 118,
    194

JAMES, WILLIAM, 153, 181, 200
Johnson, Dr., 61, 66, 104, 107, 187
Jowett, Dr., 173
Judgment, types of, 92

KANT, 5, 6, 64, 82–99
    and God, 96, 173
    and Hegel, 95, 98
    and Hume, 87
    and Leibniz, 48, 50, 94
Kepler, 4, 135
Keynes, J. M., 73, 146, 147
Kirchhoff, 146

LA METTRIE, 136
Language, 10, 11, 53, 54, 69, 90,
    157, 179
Laplace, 36
Laws of logic, 174, 180
    of Nature, 41, 72, 163, 170, 175,
    181, 182, 183, 190, 192
Leibniz, 4, 28, 35, 39, 66, 86, 132,
    187
    and epistemology, 48, 49
    and God, 47, 50
    and Newton, 44, 50
    and monads, 40, 46–49, 159
    and substance, 46, 76
Lenin, 4, 121, 125, 127, 129, 146
Leucippus, 19
Levy, Hyman, 121
Lewis, C. I., 184, 191, 192, 193, 198
Locke, 4, 5, 6, 28, 51, 52, 65, 118,
    141
    and Berkeley, 63, 68, 69, 72
    and general ideas, 54, 67, 68, 84
    and Leibniz, 53
    and Newton, 53

Locke and probability, 62, 63
    and qualities, 57, 61, 62
    and simple ideas, 58, 60, 61
    and substance, 61, 158, 169
Logical atomism, 46, 50, 155, 170,
    179, 189
    constants, 174
    Positivism, 5, 73, 121, 178, 182–
    184, 197

MACH, 146, 178
Maimonides, 41
Mana, 14
Marx, 120, 121, 122, 126, 129, 130,
    151
Mass, 30
Material cause, 23
Materialism, 13, 19, 20, 21
    Dialectical, 5, 18, 121–133, 149,
    151
    Emergent, 183, 195
    Mechanical, 31, 32, 36, 118, 112,
    132, 136, 137, 147, 150, 153,
    162, 194, 195
Materialism and Empirio-Criticism
    (Lenin), 121
Matter, 22, 23, 32, 36, 61
    and Berkeley, 71, 150
    and Engels, 124, 125
    and Mill, 143
    and Russell, 177
Mathematics, 7, 32, 44, 62, 90,
    152, 171, 172
    and empiricism, 75, 76, 81, 144,
    146
    and logic, 127, 155, 179, 180
    and mysticism, 17, 177
McDougall, W., 50
Meaning, 180, 196
Metaphysics, 52, 64, 80, 98, 141,
    146, 156, 166
    method of, 7, 39, 56, 180, 181, 196
    systems of, 18, 38–64, 100–133
Mechanics, 146
Mill, J. S., 140, 143–146, 182
Middle Ages, 3, 24
Mind, 9, 20
    and body, 34, 42, 176, 177, 184
Mind and the World Order (Lewis),
    86, 184, 191
Mode, 42, 92
Modes of Thought (Whitehead), 158
Monad, 40, 46–50, 159
Monadology, 53, 66, 132

Monism, 36, 37, 41, 49, 102, 123, 177
Moore, G. E., 178
Moral Law, 97
Morgan, Lloyd, 153
Motion, 25, 79, 146, 151, 152, 190
Mysticism and Logic (Russell), 80

NEURATH, O., 178
Newton, 4, 30, 44, 50, 56, 65, 67, 79, 139, 140, 146, 181
Nominalism, 10, 30, 54
Noumena, 93, 94, 98
Number, 17, 20, 45, 50, 71, 125, 159, 170, 171

OCCAM, 36
Order of Nature, 40, 41, 102, 194
Organism, 46, 155
Origin of Species (Darwin), 151

PARMENIDES, 18, 19, 20, 105, 109, 117
Pascal, 65
Peano, 178
Pearson, Karl, 146
Peirce, Charles, 181
Percepts, 67, 79, 82, 84, 86, 89, 175, 177
Persia, 13, 16
Phenomena, 48, 93, 98, 106, 146
Philosophy, 2, 105, 117, 182
    experimental, 4, 30, 35, 38, 138
    progress of, 5, 7, 100, 193
    speculative, 4, 157
Philosophy of Hegel, The (Stace), 115
Philosophy and Logical Syntax (Carnap), 181
Philosophy for a Modern Man, A (Levy), 128
Philosophy and the Physicists (Stebbing), 8
Plato, 3, 5, 6, 24, 105, 162
    theory of ideas, 20, 21, 31, 83, 98, 103
Pluralism, 49
Poincaré, H., 199
Pope, Alexander, 65, 66
Positivism, 136, 143, 146, 156, 171
Potential, 24, 114
Pragmatism, 181, 182, 196, 200
Principia (Newton), 56
Principles of Human Knowledge (Berkeley), 66, 72

Principia Mathematica (Russell and Whitehead), 155, 171
Process, 16, 25, 125, 159, 160
Process and Reality (Whitehead), 10, 23, 156, 165
Probability, 62, 63, 142, 143, 182
Progress, 120, 125, 151, 153
Prolegomena to an Idealist Theory of Knowledge (N. Kemp Smith), 58
Propositions, 24, 69, 106, 109, 167, 168, 171, 180
    elementary, 179, 181
    factual, 77, 89, 96
    formal, 93, 96, 168
Propositional functions, 172, 174
Pythagoras, 17–20, 27, 177

QUALITY, 22, 57, 61, 109, 125, 140, 146
    emergent, 153, 154, 161
    empirical, 29, 92, 154, 161
    occult, 56
    primary and secondary, 30, 36, 48, 57, 61, 157
    and quantity, 122, 126, 128, 151
Quantum theory, 8, 155

RADICAL physicalism, 178
Rationalism (*see also* Metaphysics):
    deductive, 7, 18, 35, 39, 51, 56, 83, 95, 117, 143, 193
    Greek, 28
    modern (*see also* Empiricism), 40, 122
Reality, 10, 21, 39, 72, 77, 93, 103, 104, 117, 152, 193
Realism, 9, 129, 176, 191
Reason, 3, 14, 15, 40
    and commonsense, 28, 29, 48, 74, 141, 146
    and Hegel, 114
    and Kant, 95
    and science, 137, 189
    worship of, 135, 136
Relations, 94, 160, 162, 170, 174
Relativity, Theory of, 6, 94, 158
Religion, 6, 13, 73, 96, 115, 132, 137, 150, 161, 200
Religion in the Making (Whitehead), 161
Russell, Bertrand, 9, 141, 144, 167–178, 197
    and Berkeley, 4, 176

Russell and Bergson, 152, 171
  and Causation, 80, 175, 198
  and Hume, 174, 176
  and Kant, 171
  and Logical Positivism, 121, 178
  and Solipsism, 187
  and Theory of Descriptions, 168, 172
Rousseau, 136

Sceptical Essays (Russell), 9
Schelling, 100
Schlick, M., 178, 182
Scholasticism, 3, 30, 53, 65, 199
Schopenhauer, 105
Science, 13, 30, 134, 135, 141, 181, 199
  and philosophy, 2, 31, 56, 64, 81, 132, 134, 183
  and method of, 31, 38, 39, 137, 138, 139, 140, 187–190
Science and Human Experience (Dingle), 187
Science and the Modern World (Whitehead), 156, 157, 159
Scientific Thought (Broad), 37
Science versus Idealism (Cornforth), 121
Secret of Hegel, The (J. H. Stirling), 120
Self and Berkeley, 70, 72
  and Descartes, 34, 77
  and Dingle, 188
  and Hume, 63, 64, 78
  and Indian philosophy, 33, 78
  and Kant, 98
  and Locke, 66
  and Logical Positivism, 183
  and Russell, 176, 177
  and Wittgenstein, 191
Sensation, 58, 60, 85, 91
Sense-data, 69, 75, 197
Shaw, G. B., 153
Similarity, 85
Socrates, 27
Solipsism, 47, 72, 85, 106, 176, 187, 191, 198
Soul, 33
Soviet Union, 5, 121
Space, 25, 44, 48, 50, 91, 94, 158, 160
Space–time, 154, 159, 161, 162
Space, Time and Deity (Alexander), 154

Spencer, Herbert, 150, 151, 152
Spinoza, 27, 28, 35, 39, 118, 137
  and ethics, 43
  and God, 40, 41, 42
  and Leibniz, 44, 45, 48
Stebbing, L. Susan, 8, 73
Steele, 65
Sublation, 114
Subject and object, 106, 108, 109, 110
Substance, 45, 63, 68, 76, 84
  and accidents, 24, 61, 151
  and attributes, 22, 33, 36, 44, 102
  and causation, 158, 175
  and God, 40, 42
  and Ionians, 14, 15, 16
  and Monads, 46
  self-moving, 123, 125, 126
Substratum, 24, 61, 71, 106, 158, 169
Synthetic judgments, 77, 90, 171
Synthesis, 114, 122

Tautology, 174, 180
Teleology, 125
Thales, 6, 15
Théodicée (Leibniz), 66
Thesis, 114
Things and events, 159
  and ideas, 71, 75, 104, 123
  and process, 16, 25, 125
  as states of substance, 42, 45
  in themselves, 48, 50, 94, 103, 146
Time, 6, 91, 149
  absolute, 44
  atomic, 41, 160
  as relation, 25, 48, 50, 94, 161
Toland, 65
Tractatus Logico-Philosophicus (Wittgenstein), 178
Treatise of Human Nature, A (Hume), 74
Truth, 25, 59, 71, 143, 198, 199
  and coherence, 42
  and correspondence, 77
  and logic, 76, 101, 174, 179, 182, 197
  and Marxism, 123, 128–131
  and mathematics, 90, 144

Uniformity of nature, 79, 102, 144
Unity of opposites, 16, 109, 114

Universal Philosophy, 105, 117

Universals, 21, 22, 30, 54, 55, 67, 82, 103, 104, 107

Unknowable, the, 93, 94, 98, 101, 150

VERIFICATION, 138, 179, 181, 182, 198

Vienna Circle, 178

Vitalism, 24

Voltaire, 136

WALLACE, WILLIAM, 105

Whitehead, A. N., 9, 150, 156–166, 197
  and Bergson, 160
  and Extensive Abstraction, 171, 172
  and God, 164, 165, 166
  and Leibniz, 51, 159
  and perception, 157, 163, 168
  and simple location, 159

Wittgenstein, 50, 174, 178, 190, 198

Worcester, Bishop of, 62

Words, 54, 55, 67, 70

ZENO, 6, 105, 152